Barrier of a Common Language

POETS ON POETRY

David Lehman, General Editor
Donald Hall, Founding Editor

New titles

Dana Gioia, *Barrier of a Common Language*
Karl Shapiro, *Essay on Rime*
Charles Simic, *The Metaphysician in the Dark*
William Stafford, *The Answers Are Inside the Mountains*

Recently published

Thomas M. Disch, *The Castle of Perseverance*
Mark Jarman, *Body and Soul*
Philip Levine, *So Ask*
David Mura, *Song for Uncle Tom, Tonto, and Mr. Moto*
Stephen Yenser, *A Boundless Field*

Also available are collections by

A. R. Ammons, Robert Bly, Philip Booth, Marianne Boruch,
Hayden Carruth, Fred Chappell, Amy Clampitt, Tom Clark,
Douglas Crase, Robert Creeley, Donald Davie, Peter Davison,
Tess Gallagher, Suzanne Gardinier, Linda Gregerson,
Allen Grossman, Thom Gunn, Rachel Hadas, John Haines,
Donald Hall, Joy Harjo, Robert Hayden, Edward Hirsch,
Daniel Hoffman, Jonathan Holden, John Hollander,
Andrew Hudgins, Josephine Jacobsen, Weldon Kees, Galway Kinnell,
Mary Kinzie, Kenneth Koch, John Koethe, Yusef Komunyakaa,
Richard Kostelanetz, Maxine Kumin, Martin Lammon (editor),
Philip Larkin, David Lehman, Philip Levine, Larry Levis,
John Logan, William Logan, William Matthews, William Meredith,
Jane Miller, Carol Muske, Geoffrey O'Brien, Gregory Orr,
Alicia Suskin Ostriker, Ron Padgett, Marge Piercy, Anne Sexton,
Charles Simic, Louis Simpson, William Stafford, Anne Stevenson,
May Swenson, James Tate, Richard Tillinghast, Diane Wakoski,
C. K. Williams, Alan Williamson, Charles Wright, and James Wright

Dana Gioia

Barrier of a Common Language

AN AMERICAN LOOKS
AT CONTEMPORARY
BRITISH POETRY

Ann Arbor

THE UNIVERSITY OF MICHIGAN PRESS

2006   2005   2004   2003   4   3   2   1

A CIP catalog record for this book is available from the British Library.

Library of Congress Cataloging-in-Publication Data

Gioia, Dana.
   Barrier of a common language : an American looks at
contemporary British poetry / Dana Gioia.
      p.   cm. — (Poets on poetry)
   Includes index.
   ISBN 0-472-09582-X (Cloth : alk. paper) — ISBN 0-472-06582-3
(Paper : alk. paper)
   1. English poetry—20th century—History and criticism.   2.
English poetry—21st century—History and criticism.   3. English
poetry—Appreciation—United States.   4. English
language—Versification.   I. Title.   II. Series.
PR611 .G565   2003
821'.9109—dc21   2003005041

For Frederick Morgan and Paula Deitz
Not merely great editors but absolute angels

Contents

Preface

"I feel very much the need to be on the periphery of
things."

　　　　　　　　　　　　　　　　　　—Philip Larkin

The essays in this book grew out of a conviction that American
and English poetry remain inextricably connected. While this
belief is hardly controversial, it is a notion now more honored in
the breach than the observance—at least in regard to contem-
porary poetry. In America the literary curriculum is still largely
based on the chronological survey of English-language texts
from Beowulf and Chaucer to the present (with a few transla-
tions of Greek classics—usually just Homer and Sophocles—
added for historical perspective). In this pedagogic model
British poetry enjoys a monopoly until the mid-nineteenth
century when Americans suddenly achieve equal billing. The
two poetries maintain an uneasy balance for about a hundred
years. Then in the decades after the Second World War British
poetry—like the British Empire itself—seems suddenly to be
swept away and vanishes. The story of English-language poetry,
therefore, implicitly concludes with American verse triumphant
and all-powerful. A stirring tale perhaps but not an accurate one.

The reasons for British poetry's vanishing act are both prac-
tical and political. In practical terms, there is so much contem-
porary verse to read that American teachers, critics, and an-
thologists justifiably feel a need to focus their efforts. In such a
situation their own country's efforts tend to receive priority. In
political terms, there has long been a sense of triumphalism in
the study of modern American poetry. Although the notion is
rarely articulated openly, there is a tacit assumption in most an-
thologies and criticism that in the past century American po-
etry—vigorous, innovative, and bold—decisively vanquished its

safe, tired, and tame British counterpart. (In the American account, only Irish poets escaped the general holocaust. Canadians, Australians, South Africans, and other Anglophonic poets don't even merit a mention.) Modernism was the glory of American verse, the story runs, and the future belongs to us.

Recently the multicultural movement has critiqued some elements of American literary triumphalism, but its remedy was not a rapprochement with contemporary British writing. Instead, the answer was to incorporate postcolonial English-language works, especially from the Third World, into literary and academic culture—a sensible strategy but an incomplete one. This effort has succeeded in adding some notable African, Caribbean, and Asian writers to the canon, though few of them are poets, but it leaves the English issue unanswered. What is the current relationship between American poetry and that of our language's Mother country?

The effects of the gradual but drastic break between the American and British poetic traditions are many, but the most obvious and pernicious has been simple ignorance. American literati no longer read new British poetry. American anthologists rarely include contemporary works from the United Kingdom. Poetic reputations now seldom cross the Atlantic. Consequently, knowledgeable American readers of contemporary poetry often don't even recognize the names of living British poets. Usually the only English poets who achieve much literary fame in America are the ones like Thom Gunn and Geoffrey Hill, who resettle here. (This strategy, however, has not yet been equally successful for Tony Connor and Dick Davis.) For someone like myself, who believes there are many enormously accomplished British poets writing at present, this neglect seems both unfortunate and unnecessary.

When I first noticed this situation nearly thirty years ago, I assumed it was temporary. No powerful new generation had yet appeared to challenge the eminence of older masters like Ted Hughes, Philip Larkin, Basil Bunting, and Robert Graves. But when exciting new poets like Tony Harrison, James Fenton, and Wendy Cope arrived to rapturous receptions in the U.K., they remained largely invisible here. There was simply too much domestic literary activity competing for the reader's limited time and attention. There also seemed to be a general sense that nothing the Brits did now mattered much to American poetry. I have been particularly struck by how few American poets read or discuss their British counterparts. And how fewer still ever write about them. Of the American poet-critics in my generation probably only William Logan has consistently written on current British verse.

There is much to be said in favor of reading contemporary British poetry, but let two arguments suffice for the moment. The first is pleasure. I find it hard to imagine that any avid reader who sat down for an hour with a volume by Larkin, Fenton, Cope, Kingsley Amis, or Charles Causley would not rise delighted and refreshed. English poets have not lost their talent to entertain as well as to move and enlighten. Donald Davie once claimed that the key difference between English and American poets is a sense of audience. Americans, he maintained, write from a profound sense of isolation. The English never doubt that they address an audience, however small. That sense of community often gives British poetry a companionable or public quality that seems slightly foreign but also restorative to an American. That same sense of an audience also accounts for the humor that characterizes so much of the best modern British poetry—from Thomas Hardy and A. E. Housman through W. H. Auden and Philip Larkin. It is not necessarily an easy humor. More often it is the bitter satire found in Hardy, Larkin, or Anthony Burgess, but this particularly English sensibility recognizes the need to make a dark worldview attractive to contemplate. "Deprivation is for me," joked Larkin, "what daffodils were for Wordsworth." That self-deprecating remark is not only both a good joke and ruthlessly honest self-criticism; it is also a comment no major American poet would have made. American bards are more likely to echo Walt Whitman, "I celebrate myself, and sing myself." Both literary strategies can produce magnificent results, but they are irreconcilably different.

The second argument in favor of reading new British verse is perspective. British poetry is a foreign literature that Americans can read in the original. Even if they have grown apart in the past 150 years, British and American poetry share the same root stock. Nourished by the same sources, they both resemble and differ from one another in interesting and significant ways. To see what British poets take from American literature teaches us something about ourselves, just as understanding what currently fashionable ideas they ignore challenges our own aesthetic assumptions. Aside from its strictly artistic achievements, British poetry can be studied as a laboratory testing the imaginative possibilities of the contemporary English language.

The essays in this book were written mostly with the purpose of introducing some interesting new poets to an American audience. Many of the essays reflect a spirit of advocacy—an attempt to make a compelling case for the reader's attention. I have had the considerable advantage of writing here mostly about poets I admire. Advocacy and admiration, however, are no substitutes for critical candor and objectivity, so I have often discussed a particular poet's failings as well as his or her achievements. Such mixed evaluations seem to infuriate some readers, who want an author praised (or attacked) unreservedly. It is silly, however, to insist that a critic must accept or reject a poet's total *oeuvre* rather than judging each individual work by its particular merits. Few writers manage a consistently high level of accomplishment. (Even Larkin's astonishing consistency of achievement was qualified once his unpublished and uncollected verse was presented.) And some genuinely important poets like Graves and Hughes were so prolific and uneven that they can best be championed selectively. Even in advocacy, a critic's task is not to praise but to praise rightly.

I wrote the essays and reviews that make up this book over the past twenty years—not intending at first to collect them in a single volume. Once I put them together, I then painstakingly rewrote several of the essays both to incorporate new material and to refine their arguments. Distracted by other obligations, I worked so slowly that I was sure similar volumes would supercede my study of contemporary British poetry. I am both sorry and surprised to say that I was wrong. Two or three scholarly volumes have discussed the older generation of British poets, but no American poet-critic has yet to publish a similar survey. However brief and belated, this book still fills a necessary gap.

The Barrier of a Common Language

New British Poetry in the Eighties

Even fifty years ago it would have been inconceivable for an American interested in contemporary poetry to ignore British verse. Hardy, Lawrence, and Bridges were only recently dead; Housman, de la Mare, and Kipling still active elder presences. Yeats was writing at the dizzying height of his power. Graves had emerged as a mature talent. Meanwhile an exciting group of younger poets, including Auden, MacNeice, Spender, Thomas, and Empson, had just broken onto the scene. American poetry may have achieved its difficult independence, but the ties to the mother country remained strong. Not to know what was being written in Britain was, very simply, not to be well-versed. Poetry in English was still widely seen as an unbroken continuum starting in the British Isles and stretching to America and beyond. And if our most celebrated poet, T. S. Eliot, lived in London and spoke with a British accent, that did not seem altogether odd.

Today the situation has changed so drastically that most American readers are not only unfamiliar with current British poetry, but modestly proud of the fact. They do not dissemble, but instead urbanely flourish their ignorance as an indisputable sign of discrimination. The clear if unstated implication is that they have concentrated on more relevant aspects of literature. If British poetry has not yet sunk in the American literary consciousness to the marginal status of Canadian or South African verse, it has unquestionably receded to the second rank. Like current Italian theater or German fiction, it is viewed as an interesting but peripheral subject.

From the *Hudson Review* 37 (spring 1984): 6–20.

Explaining the dramatic change in our receptivity to British poetry could be the subject of an interesting book. Certainly there were literary reasons—most notably the lack of British poets with internationally acknowledged reputations and the continuing rivalry between English and American poetic schools. Auden's move to America and Thomas's early death robbed Britain of its two most celebrated talents, and no equally prominent poets rose to take their places. Indeed at present one of the most conspicuous features of the English literary landscape is the absence of any actively presiding elder poets like Yeats or Eliot whose major accomplishments are generally recognized. The three older poets whose work seems most guaranteed to survive (Basil Bunting, Robert Graves, and Philip Larkin) have all stopped writing—not only poetry but prose—and they have all long since left the literary scene. The once prolific Graves has been silenced by senility, Bunting by age mixed with alcohol, and Larkin like Eliot before him by the magnitude of his own reputation.

Among middle-aged English poets only Ted Hughes commands an international audience, and a few others like Geoffrey Hill, Charles Tomlinson, and Thom Gunn have small but loyal American followings (although Gunn hardly counts as an Englishman, having lived in the U.S. for thirty years). The few remaining poets with American reputations—like Donald Davie and Kingsley Amis—are known primarily for their prose. The implication here is not that Britain lacks poets of major stature, only that since Auden and Thomas few of them have managed to build significant reputations outside the United Kingdom. Even poets of the stature of Tomlinson, Davie, Hill, as well as R. S. Thomas, C. H. Sisson, and Charles Causley, remain little read abroad.

This isolation is not accidental but the result of both British design and American disdain. The mainstream of British poetry over the past thirty years has tried to minimize foreign influence and assert its specifically national character. "The Movement," for example, Britain's most influential poetic group of the fifties, stressed the native features of the English poetic tradition and treated Modernism as an ephemeral imported aberration, thereby rejecting many of the assumptions which had temporarily united Anglo-American poetry. Likewise the development of regional poetic movements in the United Kingdom, especially among distinct national groups like the Scottish or Welsh, has too often resulted in a parochial kind of poetry unlikely to interest overseas readers.

Meanwhile America has developed an increasingly chauvinistic and contemptuous attitude toward British poetry. This prejudice, which is rooted in the polemics of Modernist writers like William Carlos Williams who struggled for a specifically American poetic idiom, identifies British poetry with the outdated traditions which have historically repressed our native genius. In its current form this attitude asserts that all English poets are overly civilized, hopelessly conservative, and intentionally minor—incapable, in short, of the broad vision and fiery passion of their American counterparts. Needless to say, this is a very comfortable assumption for Americans to hold—rather like the theory that most Russian missiles would suffer mechanical breakdown in the event of a thermonuclear war. The demotion of British poetry has been further aided by the recent internationalization of American poetic taste. As our writers increasingly turn to the poetry of the non-English-speaking world for inspiration—especially Latin America and Eastern Europe—England has gradually lost its special position as our international partner in literature.

Although there are many important literary factors behind it, the failure of dialogue between American and British poetry is also the result of much larger political and economic changes. As America emerged from the Second World War the undisputed political and economic force in the world, it grew proudly self-sufficient in its intellectual concerns and increasingly patronizing to Britain, an attitude the English rightfully resented. At the same time Britain, financially impoverished by the war and politically enervated by the gradual loss of its empire, entered a difficult period of reassessment. Neither situation fostered an era of perceptive mutual understanding in any field, including poetry. Although the two countries remained indissolubly linked by language, history, and values, the precise nature of the relationship had become painfully problematic.

Whatever the reasons, American and British poetry have in

the last forty years begun evolving into two different literatures. Their traditions still overlap, but they are no longer even approximately identical. Their poets view both the usable past and their present agenda very differently. This divergence has not been much discussed, but it is almost universally felt each time a reader in one country picks up a new poem from the other. However good or bad, simple or complex the poem may seem, the reader knows he or she is missing a fundamental part of its meaning. He or she senses certain barriers to comprehension which the author did not intend. These barriers are linguistic, but not primarily caused by obvious factors like differing accents and vocabularies. Rather they result from deeper linguistic difficulties of two poetic languages shaped by different principles and used for dissimilar ends.

Therefore, while there are significant differences in idiom and vocabulary between American and British English, these in themselves pose no major obstacles. As anyone who has studied a foreign literature knows, one needn't understand every word to appreciate a poem. The difficulty an American faces in approaching contemporary British poetry is in hearing it accurately. "We have," as Dylan Thomas said, "the barrier of a common language." The words are familiar, but they seem arranged by some alien musical system. The two literatures have now reached a point where, as Donald Davie has pointed out, "the American reader can't hear the British poet, neither his rhythm nor his tone." This difficulty isn't only a matter of different accent and inflections, though they contribute. It is a result of two poetries developing for decades along separate lines with little communication. The assumptions a British poet now makes about his or her self, language, work, and audience are subtly different from those of an American writer. He or she is not merely writing in a foreign accent. The poem that is being created is now in some ways a foreign text. An American remains a privileged translator, but a translator nonetheless.

This inability to hear British verse may explain why literate Americans have abandoned current English poetry, but not drama, cinema, popular music, or television, where performance bridges the widening gap between the artist and his or her transatlantic audience. In those art forms an American literally can hear the tone and rhythm of the language—usually reinforced by gesture. Likewise British novels have remained accessible since the form is compendious enough to provide sufficient context for its own interpretation. But poetry, the most compressed literary form, the one most dependent on the economy and precision of its language, has become a disadvantaged genre abroad. Whether it ever regains the importance in Anglo-American literary relations it had fifty years ago will depend on the quality of service it receives from critics, poets, editors, and anthologists, who alone can make it accurately heard and understood.

Anthologies provide the easiest access for American readers into contemporary British poetry, and the lack of reliable contemporary anthologies on both sides of the Atlantic may account for a large part of the apathy and misunderstanding between the two literatures. Therefore the recent publication of two serious selections of young British poets will be of particular interest to American readers. The first of these anthologies is *Contemporary British Poetry,* edited by Blake Morrison and Andrew Motion, published late in 1982 by Penguin. Although this collection was met with generally bad reviews, it filled such an important need in attempting to define the younger generation of poets that it became, *de facto,* the standard anthology of the current scene.

Making sense out of the current superabundance of young poets is no easy task, and the Morrison/Motion team deserves commendation for the considerable work that must have gone into their project, but their anthology is not without serious flaws. The major problem is their critical apparatus. Their introduction begins with the bold rhetoric of the literary manifesto. Their claims are so general that the time could just as easily be 1922 as 1982:

> There are points in literary history when decisive shifts of sensibility occur. New, usually aggressive notes are struck; conventions are challenged or broken or simply exposed as being conventions; innovations of form accompany the

> broaching of unfamiliar subject matter. . . . Such a shift of sen-
> sibility has taken place very recently in British poetry. . . . A
> body of work has been created which demands, for its appre-
> ciation, a reformation of poetic taste.

Who wouldn't buy an anthology which promised such a transformation? Reading this assertive opening, one expects to turn the pages and find "new styles of architecture, a change of heart," poems as explosively new as the early *Cantos* or *The Bridge* seemed half a century ago. Instead one encounters twenty very accessible poets, whose work is contemporary without being particularly innovative. The predominant influences are Auden and Larkin—not bad models to be sure, but hardly ones requiring "a reformation of poetic taste."

Unfortunately, the introduction's critical problems don't end there, and its stylistic ones only begin. Adopting an omniscient editorial *we* and lapsing into chic academic jargon (their favorite adjective is *ludic*), the editors start establishing the qualities of the new poetic sensibility, few of which bear much relation to the poems they have included. For example, they gratuitously announce that "the new poetry" rejects "the received idea of the poet as the-person-next-door" (presumably a slap at Larkin). Why then have they included among their opening selections four very straightforward poems by Douglas Dunn and another by Hugo Williams, which literally do discuss the people next door? Likewise a little later they state that the new sensibility has "been antipathetic to the production of candidly personal poetry," a principle implicitly refuted by the many excellent personal poems they then include. The problem is simply that Morrison and Motion have tried to define a unified poetic generation where none exists, and in trying to reduce a very diverse collection of poets into a few impressive generalizations they have become blinded by their own abstractions. Not surprisingly, amid all the manifesto rhetoric, the real news in their introduction gets lost, namely that after a rather barren stretch, British poetry is beginning to renew itself. They share the feeling, pervasive in England, that the sixties and early seventies were a wasteland for new poets. Overwhelmed by pop music, radical politics, American poetics, and class consciousness, British poetry entered what Neil Powell has called "that other 'low dishonest decade.'" Now in the eighties, as Morrison and Motion demonstrate in their selections, a new generation of writers has emerged whose talent is matched in integrity and self-assurance.

If Morrison and Motion's enthusiasm for their generation temporarily blinded their critical faculties, luckily it left their editorial abilities largely intact, for *Contemporary British Poetry* is generally an exciting and engaging collection—if also somewhat uneven. Of the twenty poets included only four strike me as marginal or mediocre—Penelope Shuttle, David Sweetman, Carol Rumens, and Medbh McGuckian. If one also excludes the charming but slight Hugo Williams, that leaves fourteen poets of real substance represented by generally good selections which convey the quality and variety of their work. By current American standards this ratio makes the Penguin book a superb anthology, though that may seem like damning with faint praise.

Morrison and Motion divide their poets into four slightly overlapping groups—the Northern Irish, the "Martians," the working class, and the narrative. To an American reader these unfamiliar groupings are simply one more sign of how foreign British poetry has become, but to the English they express the editors' literary politics. There are, for example, no Welsh or Scottish poets (except Douglas Dunn, who is in some ways becoming more English than the English). Many British readers may feel this omission reflects the editors' London/Belfast bias (though perhaps the editors were honestly unable to find any young Welsh or Scottish poets of sufficient quality—it is difficult for an American to judge). A more obvious omission, however, is the absence of any of the Carcanet poets, the group of young neo-formalist poets clustered around Carcanet Press in Manchester, who form one of the most interesting literary movements in England today. The omission of such a distinguished and influential group was surely deliberate, and reflects a very real but seldom mentioned ideological rivalry in English letters between London and the provinces (in this case Manchester), a situation not unlike the contention in American poetry between New York and the Midwest. Unfortunately this omission also makes the new Penguin anthology unrepresentative despite its other strengths.

The Northern Irish group makes a very strong impression, particularly Seamus Heaney, Derek Mahon, Tom Paulin, and Michael Longley. As Morrison and Motion point out, Belfast has been as central to the new poetry as London. Somehow the tragic political forces at work in Northern Ireland have created a poetic generation of broad vision and intense identity. Seamus Heaney needs no introduction in America, but it is surprising that Mahon, who is almost Heaney's equal, is not better known. He is one of the best young poets now writing in English. Readers of *Contemporary British Poetry* will want to supplement its selections with Mahon's retrospective *Poems: 1962–1978*. They should also look at Paulin's most recent collection, *The Strange Museum*. These books masterfully reveal that particularly Irish gift of fusing individual and political concerns. The poems reflect the social realities of Ireland without ever betraying the integrity of each author's individual vision. For example, in Paulin's "Second-Rate Republics," political metaphors are so skillfully used to characterize a couple's sexual relationship that the poem begins to take on both a psychological and a social meaning:

> He touches her and she sees herself
> Being forced back into a shabby city
> Somewhere else in Europe: how clammy
> It is, how the crowds press and slacken
> On the pavement, shaking photographs
> Of a statesman's curdled face.
>
> Now there is only a thin sheet
> Between their struggling bodies
> And the stained mattress.
> Now his face hardens like a photograph,
> And in the distance she hears
> The forced jubilance of a crowd
> That is desolate and obedient.

At the moment the biggest news in British poetry is the "Martian" school, a group of young poets headed by Craig Raine and

Christopher Reid, and well represented in the Penguin anthology. This fashionable gang owes its extraterrestrial sobriquet to James Fenton, who, when his friends Raine and Reid shared the *New Statesman*'s poetry prize, pointed out the unusual stylistic traits they had in common. Borrowing the central conceit from Raine's prize-winning "A Martian Sends a Postcard Home," Fenton summarized their mission as an attempt to make the reader see the familiar world in an alien way, especially by using bizarre metaphors for everyday objects.

Book reviewers love nothing more than a new school of poetry. It gives some shape, however illusory, to the depressingly vague mass of contemporary verse that crosses their desks. Not surprisingly, therefore, no sooner had Raine and Reid been playfully nicknamed "Martians" than the term worked its way into general critical parlance. Reviewers fiercely debated the merits of the so-called school, and for a while any poet who ventured a fancy metaphor was comfortably pigeonholed. The resulting publicity made Raine and Reid famous in the attention-starved world of poetry. Their books sold; their poems were anthologized; their imitators proliferated; and Raine, the undisputed leader of the group, emerged as the most influential poet of his generation—not only the E.T. of English poetry but its Audie Murphy as well, having won nearly every honor and award short of the Laureateship.

A skeptical reader might justifiably complain that there is nothing especially new in the Martian theory of poetry, their method being only the latest variation of the many *Entfremdung* techniques that have characterized modern literature. But poetic theory ultimately matters very little and practice very much. And in their practice Raine and Reid have created a tangibly new and different poetry, even if the differences are more of degree than of kind. How is this possible in a period when the average poem is bloated with imagery and metaphor? The Martians' metaphorical density and ingenuity of language are not in themselves as new as their ability to use these characteristics to produce poems of suave and graceful transparency. Their best poems are extraordinarily rich without being cloying. Likewise if critics complain that the "Martian" aim of making the familiar world seem new is the traditional mission of poetic metaphor, this too is to be expected. All poetic schools earn their reputations by announcing old truths as new discoveries and claiming private patents on general techniques.

For a sample of the novel way Raine handles his metaphors and language, here are a few lines from the movement's *Urtext,* "A Martian Sends a Postcard Home":

> Mist is when the sky is tired of flight
> and rests its soft machine on ground:
>
> then the world is dim and bookish
> like engravings under tissue paper.
>
> Rain is when the earth is television.
> It has the property of making colours darker.
> . . . .
> But time is tied to the wrist
> or kept in a box, ticking with impatience.

If Raine's importance has been overrated by the media, it has also been underestimated by his critics. He is a remarkably inventive poet with a fine ear. The problem with his work—and indeed that of the whole Martian school—is not so much one of present performance but future development. The poetry is often bright, fresh, and entertaining; the question is, how long will it remain so? How long can the "Martian" style be exploited before it becomes tired and predictable? How long can metaphor alone command a reader's attention and hide the frequently mundane content of the poetry? As one critic mused, "Metaphor as a way of life. One wonders if it is quite enough."

Raine himself must sense these limitations, for his latest work, *A Free Translation,* shows him tentatively broadening his scope. While this small pamphlet may not mark a new stage in his career, it does reflect a difficult maturation. These six new poems, all written in thin three-line stanzas, are quieter and more somber than his early work. The sharp metaphors are still there but less densely, and they no longer serve as the driving forces of the poem. Most important, however, Raine now shows more personal involvement in his material, more humanity in his approach. As the *enfant terrible* has become a family man, he seems more keenly aware of the responsibilities people have toward one another. But while this humanity adds weight to Raine's poetry, he has not yet mastered it as distinctively as he has imagery and metaphor. *A Free Translation* is a curious book. It contains much wonderful writing but no whole poems as captivating as his best earlier work. Almost every line works well, and yet the poems as a whole are disappointing. They are not bad, just not good enough.

While Christopher Reid has also won many awards from the British poetic establishment, he, unlike Raine, has served as the whipping boy of anti-Martian critics. Reid, they claim (not without justification), is a "dandy," an irresponsible aesthete who delights in exotic language and improbable fictions. He lacks, in short, the high seriousness which all right-thinking Anglo-Saxons look for in poetry. These accusations are all indisputably true. Reid is an unabashedly minor poet in an era which demands major gestures. And yet along with James Fenton and John Ash he strikes me as one of the most imaginative and entertaining young poets in England.

Those who accept Auden's theory that the most promising young poet is not the earnest chap with the message but the one who likes to hang around words and see what they're up to will immediately understand Reid's appeal. His work seems motivated almost solely by his delight in language. In his best poems the world becomes not only new but joyfully appealing. The rings left by a wet coffee cup are transformed into Zen calligraphy, or an ordinary recipe for soup becomes a playful sacrifice to the household gods, and in "Zeugma," the final poem of his new collection *Pea Soup,* a rhetorical figure turns into a metaphor for both love and poetry.

> We are two words set free
> from the common dictionary,
> to act with a new, *ad hoc* complicity.
>
> Our only go-between, "and,"
> carries its contraband
> in a package the unpoetic may not understand.

Working-class is a meaningful term to apply to some British poets, since in the United Kingdom class distinctions involving not only values but also language still remain strongly defined. From a sociological standpoint many of the poets in the Penguin anthology (and in the Carcanet collection to be discussed later) are working-class, but two of them—Tony Harrison and Douglas Dunn—are notable for the skilled intensity with which they deal with the complex problems of their class origins and identities. Harrison, whose work is completely unavailable in the U.S., will be a new name to most Americans, but he is the real thing, a poet of wide range, passionate interests, and verbal dexterity who can handle strict forms in an entirely natural way. His virtues are so self-evident that one need only quote him. Here is "Marked with D.," a characteristic short poem about the death of the neighborhood baker.

> When the chilled dough of his flesh went in an oven
> not unlike those he fuelled all his life,
> I thought of his cataracts ablaze with Heaven
> and radiant with the sight of his dead wife,
> light streaming from his mouth to shape her name,
> "not Florence and not Flo but always Florrie."
> I thought how his cold tongue burst into flame
> but only literally, which makes me sorry,
> sorry for his sake there's no Heaven to reach.
> I get it all from Earth my daily bread
> but he hungered for release from mortal speech
> that kept him down, the tongue that weighed like lead.
>
> The baker's man that no one will see rise
> and England made to feel like some dull oaf
> is smoke, enough to sting one person's eyes
> and ash (not unlike flour) for one small loaf.

Douglas Dunn, the other working-class hero of the Penguin anthology, is one of the most widely read poets in England, and deservedly so. His first book, *Terry Street* (1969), which earned him an immediate reputation, is a flawed work which nonetheless makes a profound impression. Writing about his neighbors in a run-down section of Hull (an English city whose closest American equivalent would probably be Buffalo), Dunn believably captured the emotional fabric of their lives. Simple, direct, and humane, the poems overcome their occasional literary shortcomings and collectively make up a powerful composite of contemporary urban life. Most young poets would not have survived such a celebrated beginning, but Dunn had a keen sense of his own limitations. In his next three books, *The Happier Life* (1972), *Love or Nothing* (1974), and *Barbarians* (1979), he slowly developed into a poet of greater technical and thematic range, clearly establishing himself as one of the important young poets on the scene.

But after such impressive development it is disheartening to read Dunn's two latest books, one of them a curiously mixed performance, the other a dull disaster. *St. Kilda's Parliament*, the indisputably better volume, contains some fine poems, but too often it shows Dunn losing touch with the sources of his own strength. Up until this volume Dunn's working-class Scottish background provided him with a unique perspective on the subjects he discussed. He could understand and identify with the English poor of Terry Street without losing his own objectivity, or write about French culture without sounding out of register. Now he seems determined to create tightly rhymed poems of sophisticated wit, a very high-flown English ambition most unsuited to his down-to-earth Scottish talent. These poems show a great deal of honest effort, but they inevitably sound forced and awkward—like Ted Hughes trying to imitate Sir John Betjeman.

In this volume Dunn has also tried to master a stream-of-consciousness poem through several ingenious verse reveries which recreate the complex turns of his mind in various situations. Dunn must have poured his notebooks into these poems, for they often sparkle line by line with captivating images, engaging metaphors, and unexpected turns of phrase. The trouble is that all but one of them fall apart under scrutiny. The notable exception is "Remembering Lunch," a controversial piece around which English reviewers are taking sides. It has already been reprinted in at least two anthologies (including the Penguin collection). One critic has called it "a long poem of indescribable dullness." But here I must agree with the Morrison/Motion contingent, for I find "Remembering Lunch" fascinating. Written in long fluent lines musically reminiscent of Ashbery at his best, the poem piles appositional phrase on phrase. But all the ornate music elaborates an argument of classical simplicity—

the virtues of solitude versus society. It is a strikingly ambitious poem, rather like a simultaneous performance of "Il Penseroso" and "L'Allegro" rearranged in a contemporary style. In general, however, *St. Kilda's Parliament* reveals broader ambitions that Dunn is only partially able to fulfill. And in the attempt to write allusive poems of wit and ideas he has abandoned the compassionate realism that was so uniquely his own, an asset of which he now seems slightly ashamed.

Despite its faults, *St. Kilda's Parliament* does contain at least half a dozen poems as good as anything Dunn has ever written, and many of its weaker ones have considerable charm. Nothing so kind can be said about his pamphlet-length poetic sequence, *Europa's Lover,* which ranks as Dunn's only dull and pretentious book. This joyless fourteen-part poem tells of Europa, an awkward symbol for European culture, sex, and inspiration, and her tiresome conversations with a sensitive young man. Luckily, no sections of *Europa's Lover* appear in the Penguin anthology, but admirers of Dunn should be forewarned.

The most captivating new poet in the Penguin anthology is James Fenton, whose second full-length book, *The Memory of War,* won almost universal admiration in the English press. For once I entirely agree with the media, as Fenton is a welcome presence—a skillful, amusing, and perceptive poet who deals deftly with both light and serious themes. Fenton, who now has one of the best jobs in the world (he is drama critic for the *London Sunday Times*), worked for several years as a political journalist in Indo-China and Germany, and these experiences appear directly in his poetry. His chief literary model is Auden, whose influence appears both in Fenton's superb technical skills and his ability to treat political themes successfully in verse. Fenton also shares some of Auden's range. He can write with equal success hilarious light verse, like his "Letter to John Fuller" (which suggests that he and Fuller enter a suicide pact to secure their poetic fame), and a haunting serious sequence like "A German Requiem." His poems on Cambodia combine the best features of poetry and journalism, and his remarkable allegory "The Skip" has the accessibility of a pop song and the integrity of a fine lyric poem. And in every style Fenton works with enviable speed and clarity.

To convey some of his versatility here are two short passages from *The Memory of War.* The first is the sonorous opening of "A German Requiem," a sequence which obliquely describes a visit to a German cemetery full of the war dead and the memories it stirs in the survivors:

> It is not what they built. It is what they knocked down.
> It is not the houses. It is the spaces between the houses.
> It is not the streets that exist. It is the streets that no longer
>   exist.
> It is not your memories which haunt you.
> It is not what you have written down.
> It is what you have forgotten, what you must forget.

And now the opening of his apocalyptic nonsense poem, "The Wild Ones," which recreates a Grade-B motorcycle gang movie with a cast of South American rodents:

> Here come the capybaras on their bikes.
> They swerve into the friendly, leafy square
> Knocking the angwantibos off their trikes,
> Giving the old-age coypus a bad scare.
> They specialise in nasty, lightning strikes.
> They leave the banks and grocers' shops quite bare,
> Then swagger through the bardoors for a shot
> Of anything the barman hasn't got.

But while these short passages demonstrate the range of Fenton's talent, they misrepresent its depth. He is a narrative and discursive poet whose real originality shows in his unexpected turns of plot and argument. Short excerpts just don't do him justice. Find someone who is going to England and make him buy you a copy of this book.

History, even literary history, moves dialectically. Thesis struggles with antithesis, anthology with anthology. Therefore it is not surprising that Michael Schmidt, publisher of Carcanet Press, whose poets were banished from the Morrison/Motion volume, would edit his own anthology. At present Schmidt is probably the most influential person on the British poetic scene. A Harvard- and Oxford-educated American who holds Mexican citizenship, he has lived for many years in Manchester, where he writes, teaches, and edits. His bimonthly magazine *PN Review* (formerly *Poetry Nation*) is one of the best poetry journals in the English-speaking world, and Carcanet Press, which he founded fifteen years ago at Oxford with a few poorly printed pamphlets, is now one of the largest literary publishers in England, with a backlist of contemporary poetry that only the venerable Faber and Faber can match. Schmidt has used these channels to foster a group of poets, mainly formalists, who are seeking to create specifically English contemporary poetry. If Auden is the presiding spirit of the Morrison/Motion contingent, Thomas Hardy and Edward Thomas are the informing presences of the Carcanet group.

Schmidt's *Some Contemporary Poets of Britain and Ireland* is not, however, a narrowly partisan anthology. He has sought to counter the imbalances of the Morrison/Motion collection with what he feels is a more representative view of younger British poets. He follows the Penguin anthology in choosing twenty poets, but his selections are very different. Only seven poets appear in both books—Peter Scupham, Tony Harrison, James Fenton, Derek Mahon, Tom Paulin, Jeffrey Wainwright, and Andrew Motion—and most of these with very different selections. Two-thirds of each book is comprised of entirely different poets. The Martians are notably absent from the Schmidt anthology (though there is a note saying that eight poems by Craig Raine were originally planned for inclusion), and popular poets like Hugo Williams and Douglas Dunn are also omitted. Certainly not only royalty difficulties are at work here, but important differences in aesthetics.

Schmidt's taste is generally of more consistent quality than Morrison and Motion's. There are no truly bad poets in his anthology, though there are a few slight ones, especially among his youngest entries like Frank Kuppner or Alison Brackenbury. But if Morrison and Motion's editorial fault is a weakness for the flip and clever, Schmidt's is a partiality toward the overly earnest. He has not only omitted most of the Penguin anthology's wittier poets, but he also represented many of his own solely through their most serious work, which limits the breadth of his otherwise catholic anthology. Schmidt also has an insatiable appetite for landscape poems, a taste matched by some of his Carcanet poets who like nothing more than to write about the English countryside. Individually most of these poems are quite fine, but by the end of the book one feels like escaping for a restful weekend in the slums. Perhaps this is a terribly American reaction. The English seem to possess more stamina in country matters.

Not surprisingly, a major component of Schmidt's anthology is a convincing selection of Carcanet poets—most notably Robert Wells, Dick Davis, Clive Wilmer, Andrew Waterman, and Jeremy Hooker. Of these Wells and Davis seem the strongest. Working within tight self-imposed constraints, they have achieved a commanding lyric intensity, as in Davis's "Semele," thematically a remarkable poem about innocence and experience, and formally a small miracle—an entirely successful contemporary sonnet:

> I imagine an English Semele—
> A gawky girl who strayed beyond the town
> Picking at stalks, alarmed by puberty . . .
> Who by the handsome stranger's side lay down
>
> And when he'd gone lay still in meadow-sweet
> Knowing herself betrayed into the world—
> Soft flesh suffused with summer's placid heat,
> The clement light in which the ferns uncurled.
>
> Both faded; meeting him again she sought
> For that half-apprehended, longed-for power—
> The glitter haunting her distracted thought
> That seemed to peer from every leaf and flower,
>
> The glory of the God . . . the girl became
> The landscape's ghost, the sunlight's edgy flame.

Schmidt's selection also has a charming surprise, namely John Ash, an accomplished experimental poet of wit and intelligence. Ash writes a very sophisticated—one is tempted to say very French—poetry in which facts and ideas are used as images to be combined into beguiling aesthetic structures. The effect is rather like reading Nabokov versified by Supervielle. His presence considerably brightens the anthology.

One of the most troubling features in both anthologies is the paucity of strong women poets. There are just five women in the Morrison/Motion collection and in Schmidt's anthology only two. Are there really so few talented young female poets in the United Kingdom, or have the editors simply missed them? Certainly the selections in the Penguin anthology are not reassuring. Of its five women poets, three seem particularly weak—though whether this impression is their fault or the editors' is difficult to say. The two remaining women—Anne Stevenson and Fleur Adcock—are very talented, but their inclusion is somewhat ironic since both of them are now in their early fifties (which makes them older than all but one of the male poets) and neither is native English. Stevenson is an American living in England, and Adcock a New Zealander who did not emigrate until she was nearly thirty. Neither of the two women Schmidt has chosen— Gillian Clarke and Alison Brackenbury—appear in the Penguin anthology, though Clarke, whose poems on the villages and countryside of her native Wales have authentic lyric sweep, deserved a place. It is a curious situation. If these two émigrés and one Welshwoman really represent the finest achievements of British women poets fifty and under, then the Muse operates very differently on the other side of the Atlantic.

If ultimately the Carcanet anthology seems more consistent than the Penguin book, it is far from definitive. Schmidt omits two of the finest poets now writing in the British Isles, Dunn and Heaney, and excludes one of the most lively new developments, the Martians. But perhaps Schmidt was not trying to be definitive. His title, *Some Contemporary Poets of England and Ireland,* hardly implies such a commitment. A reader interested in learning about the new British poetry should acquire both books. There is surprisingly little overlap, and between them one will find at least a baker's dozen diversely talented poets who stand up to any of their American contemporaries: Seamus Heaney, Tom Paulin, Derek Mahon, Dick Davis, Robert Wells, Wendy Cope, James Fenton, Tony Harrison, John Ash, Craig Raine, Christopher Reid, Peter Scupham, and—despite *Europa's*

Lover—Douglas Dunn. One must also acknowledge the talented émigrés, Fleur Adcock and Anne Stevenson. Most Americans—especially our poets—will not welcome this news. Or act on it. But the loss is mainly ours. This generation of poets has emerged without much American attention, and there is no reason to suspect that our indifference will stop them now.

The Rise of James Fenton

James Fenton's rapid rise to literary fame in the eighties served as a climax to the emergence of a new generation of English poets brought to wide attention by the publication of two influential and competitive anthologies, Blake Morrison and Andrew Motion's *Contemporary British Poetry* (1982) and Michael Schmidt's *Some Contemporary Poets of Britain and Ireland* (1983). One of the few writers prominently featured in both collections, Fenton represented to many critics the best qualities of the new wave of poets. In Seamus Heaney's canny description, the young poets were "highly self-conscious . . . anticonfessional, detached, laconic, and strangely popular considering their various devices for keeping the reader at arm's length." Fenton's literary importance, however, ultimately transcended his position as herald to a new generation. While the exuberant energy and consummate assurance of both tone and technique immediately distinguished his work, his qualities were in no way superficial. He was unsurpassed among his contemporaries in terms of range, skill, and intelligence, but it was ultimately the sheer excellence of his poetry that gradually but ineluctably earned him the position of the major British poet of his generation.

Fenton's unique accomplishment has been to create a diversity of public forms—which range from political poetry to light verse, from narrative to lyric—without compromising the integrity and concentration of his work. His mature poetry achieves an attractive balance between formal perfection and exciting, frequently unexpected content. He has employed an impressive variety of forms, from traditional rhymed stanzas to deliberately prosaic free verse. Indeed his poems are distin-

From the *Dark Horse* 8 (autumn 1999): 42–49; 9 (winter 1999–2000).

guished from those of his contemporaries by the unusually high polish of their style and the inclusive interest of their subjects. But Fenton's originality lies not so much in his formal or thematic invention as in his particular gift for combining traditional elements in powerful and often unprecedented ways. This talent has enabled him to transform moribund literary genres such as the allegory, didactic epistle, verse satire, and pastoral eclogue into vital contemporary forms. Fenton is also an unusually entertaining and intelligent poet with an ability to engage the reader's attention. He has written difficult, even obscure poems which nonetheless have proved popular and emotionally accessible. Not surprisingly, these qualities have won him an audience beyond the narrow readership of contemporary poetry.

James Martin Fenton was born in Lincoln in 1949, the son of Mary Hamilton Ingoldby Fenton and John Charles Fenton, an Anglican priest and theologian, who was also a collateral descendant of Elijah Fenton (1683–1730), a minor Augustan poet best remembered as one of Alexander Pope's collaborators in translating the *Odyssey*. Fenton's family moved twice during his childhood, first to Yorkshire and later to Lichfield, Staffordshire, the town which would provide the sinister background for his poem "A Staffordshire Murderer." At the age of nine Fenton was sent to a musical preparatory school attached to the Durham cathedral, where he was a chorister. The importance of this early musical training can hardly be overstated. Fenton's conception of poetry—except for a few early experiments—has remained steadfastly auditory and performative. Four years later he entered Repton, a public school in Derbyshire. Graduating from Repton, he spent six months at the British Institute in Florence, before starting at Magdalen College, Oxford, in 1967. At Oxford Fenton began reading in English under the tutelage of poet John Fuller, who was to become both his literary mentor and close friend. Fenton, however, soon became dissatisfied with English. Wanting to study anthropology (for which Oxford had no formal undergraduate degree), he switched to "PPP" (philosophy, psychology, physiology) as a preparatory course.

All young poets have early influences, but only a few have single ravishing passions. In a weak poet, such early fixation can stunt creative growth, but for a strong imagination *une grande passion* can focus and clarify artistic development. At Repton Fenton discovered the poetry of W. H. Auden, which would prove the most important influence on his own work. Significantly, his reading began with Auden's more didactic and discursive later work. (The first volume he read was *About the House,* which appeared in England in 1966, Fenton's last year at public school.) Auden's influence was not hard to come by at Repton, which had educated not only Auden's father but also Christopher Isherwood. Repton's church, St. Wystan's, had even inspired Auden's Christian name. The young Fenton's literary acquaintance with the work of the elder poet was reinforced by a personal encounter when Auden accepted an invitation to read at his patron saint's school. Their meeting began a sporadic friendship between the poets that lasted until Auden's death in 1973.

Fenton has defended this early infatuation with Auden as a positive influence on his development. "I think of Auden as the starting point," he told Grevel Lindop in an interview. "I was perfectly happy to imitate Auden at times and to follow what seemed to me a possible program he had set for poets, a possible area of interest they might include in their poetry, a possible way of writing a line." At Oxford he would not have been dissuaded from this program by Fuller, who at that time was writing the first version of his comprehensive and sympathetic critical manual, *A Reader's Guide to W. H. Auden* (1970). Fuller's own poetry, which is distinguished by its wit, intelligence, and technical brilliance, even offered a model of how Auden's influence could be profitably incorporated.

Like his mentors, Auden and Fuller, Fenton was remarkably precocious in his poetic development. In 1968, during his first year at Oxford, he won that year's Newdigate Prize, an award given for the best poem by an undergraduate on a set subject. His winning sonnet sequence, *Our Western Furniture,* was then broadcast on the BBC's Third Programme and published as a pamphlet by Fuller's Sycamore Press. The theme for the Newdigate competition had been set by Edmund Blunden, then the Oxford Professor of Poetry. It was "the opening of Japan, 1853–54," a subject about which the young Fenton knew nothing. With a determination and intellectual self-confidence that presaged the poet's later career in political journalism, theater reviewing, and art criticism, Fenton immersed himself in Japanese history and produced a remarkable sequence of twenty-one sonnets and two haiku (a characteristically audacious combination of disparate forms calculated to hit exactly the composition's maximum length of three hundred lines). Although awkward in spots, Fenton's sequence remains an amazing performance for a teenager, displaying both the technical proficiency and the wide-ranging intellectual interests that would become his trademarks. It also showed the beginning of the poet's fascination with besieged native cultures.

The theme of *Our Western Furniture* is the mutually incomprehensible meeting of brash imperialistic America and tottering imperial Japan in the mid–nineteenth century. The sequence loosely follows the career of Commodore Matthew Calbraith Perry, who forcibly opened Japan to foreign trade in 1853 after 250 years of almost complete isolation. Beginning just before the arrival of the American fleet in Uraga harbor, the sequence ends with Perry's death in New York in 1858. Most of the sonnets take the form of monologues by major or minor characters on both sides of the drama, including Commodore Perry, President Millard Fillmore, the first American consul to Japan, Townsend Harris, and Yezaimon, the governor of Uraga, with the ghost of the Japanese poet Basho acting as a Tiresias-like chorus.

The story of *Our Western Furniture* moves dialectically from one point of view to another, revealing how the same situations were perceived differently by Japanese and American participants. Although he does not idealize Japanese culture, Fenton's sympathies in the poem rest with Japan. (Old empires always appeal to modern poets more than new ones.) The Americans, except for Harris, are blind to the complex realities of Japan and intoxicated with a jingoistic sense of their nation's historical destiny. The Japanese, by contrast, are more sophisticated and perspicacious. Fenton underscores the differences between the cultures throughout the poem but nowhere more tellingly than in the exchange of gifts between the two sides. Unabashedly proud of their technological achievements, the Americans present a locomotive, a telegraph, and modern guns to the puzzled Japanese and receive, much to their disgust, only flowered cloth, teapots, writing instruments, and paper. This exchange foreshadows the ultimate outcome of the American intrusion. Despite their gracious ancient culture, the Japanese, as they themselves soon realize, are powerless to stop history. After the Americans land, Yezaimon reflects on America's youthful strength:

> Your newborn country's growing potency
> Bursts like spring rivers through surrounding plains.
> You pick on us as sparring partner, try
> Our strength, but find us hopeless at your game.
>
> Sensing your strengthening sinews with delight
> You give us guns, and challenge us to fight.

Around the time he was finishing *Our Western Furniture,* Fenton began another poetic experiment. His notion was to expand contemporary poetic language by finding examples of scientific writing that displayed the precision and richness of poetic diction. He assembled his discoveries both as found poems in free verse (the sequence "Exempla," in *The Memory of War*) and as traditional poems which incorporated scientific language in a manner reminiscent of Marianne Moore ("The Fruit-Grower in War Time" or "The P. H. Rivers Museum, Oxford," in *Terminal Moraine*). "In the days I was writing them," Fenton told Andrew Motion in an interview, "one of the things I found particularly seductive was scientific language, the way it used familiar words in an unfamiliar way, or completely unfamiliar words—great clusters of them, so that the mind would just have to ride for a while, while these sounds just came. That's obviously a way towards finding, in non-poetic language, what can be the poetic language of the future. . . . Poetic language is very much denatured and overworked, and it needs a new fertilizer."

Even the richest fertilizer, however, does not guarantee flowers. And Fenton's "Exempla" stands as an interesting failure; even the author now admits he considers them "heroic first attempts." However arresting in their originality, the poems in "Exempla" are ultimately dull and aridly cerebral with neither rhythmic vitality nor emotional impact. Intellectual scope and ambition, Fenton would learn—unlike many of his American contemporaries—does not guarantee imaginative vitality. Despite their shortcomings, however, the "Exempla" bear an important relationship to his mature poetry. They show that even as an undergraduate Fenton was determined to work nonliterary language and material into his poetry. The "Exempla" also demonstrate his early fascination with the clinical and objective tone of scientific writing—a very Audenesque impulse that the younger poet put to new uses. Later, Fenton would find that by employing this tone on the less recalcitrant subjects of history and politics (in poems like "Dead Soldiers" and "Chosun"), he could successfully transmute seemingly nonliterary material into striking poetry.

In 1970 Fenton graduated from Oxford after getting what he jokingly termed "the best third" in his year—"namely the most borderline." Deciding on a career in journalism, he wrote as a freelancer for six months and then in 1971 joined the staff of the *New Statesman*. Working first on the literary pages, he soon switched to politics. The next year, at the age of only twenty-two, he published his first full-length collection, *Terminal Moraine* (1972), and soon after won a Gregory Award. Wanting to become a foreign correspondent but unable to secure a position, he decided to use the Gregory money to travel to Vietnam and Cambodia as a freelance reporter. Like Auden, who had gone off to cover the Sino-Japanese War, Fenton consciously threw himself in the path of history. But unlike the elder poet, Fenton was initially unable to turn his experiences into poetry. Indeed, during the next five years, as the precocious poet became a seasoned political correspondent, he virtually stopped writing serious verse.

Arriving in Indochina in 1973, just as the American forces were withdrawing from Vietnam, Fenton witnessed the collapse of the Lon Nol regime in Cambodia and the Thieu regime in Saigon amid ongoing civil wars. Although his experiences here as a foreign correspondent would later provide the material for the political poems which catapulted him into fame with the publication of *The Memory of War* (1982) (and his 1988 volume of reportage, *All the Wrong Places*), Fenton was unable to write poetry about Indochina at the time. It would have been different, he once commented, if it had been "one's own war." But to find a war just to write about it struck him as not only artificial but disgusting. The youthful prodigy had the material, but the maturing poet needed to find the appropriate perspective.

In 1976 Fenton returned to Britain and became the *New Statesman*'s political correspondent at Westminster. Writing a weekly column on British politics over the next two years, Fenton became well-known as a left-wing journalist. At this time the *New Statesman* had also become the meeting ground for a group of younger poets who over the next two decades would dominate British poetry. This coterie included Craig Raine, Andrew Motion, Christopher Reid, and Blake Morrison—all Oxford men except Morrison. In the classic manner of a new Oxbridge generation arriving in London, this group of talented co-conspirators would play an important part in making one another's literary reputations. In 1978, however, the editorship of the *New Statesman* changed, and Fenton left to become the *Guardian*'s correspondent in Germany.

In journalistic terms Fenton's time in Germany was a failure. He found writing about Germany for a daily paper difficult, and after a year he returned to England with the intention of abandoning political journalism for good. (Fenton provided a witty account of his last days as a foreign correspondent in the introduction to *You Were Marvellous* [1983]). His tenure in Germany, however, did revive his interest in poetry. In Berlin he began sketching out an elegiac prose poem, which would eventually become "A German Requiem." At this time he also wrote his most influential piece of literary criticism, a short article entitled "Of the Martian School."

Fenton's playfully titled piece announced and defended his selection of Craig Raine and Christopher Reid as co-winners of the Prudence Farmer Award for the best poems published in the *New Statesman* during the preceding year. Discussing Raine's "A Martian Sends a Postcard Home," Fenton claimed that the Martian's alien point of view (which provides unexpected and puzzling descriptions of everyday earthly objects) was not unlike Raine's general poetic method, "which always insists on presenting the familiar at its most strange." Fenton also pointed out an affinity between Raine and Reid in their use of startling and original images. He then wittily dubbed them members of the "Martian" school, "a school that ought to be noticed, since it has enrolled two of the best poets writing in England today." Fenton need not have feared their oblivion. There are few things that British arts journalism likes more than new literary movements. The hitherto nonexistent "Martian" school of poetry was quickly noticed by the London press, which enthusiastically debated the nature and merits of its aesthetic. This unexpected broadscale publicity soon made Fenton's friends Raine and Reid two of the best-known young poets in the United Kingdom.

The year 1978 also saw the publication of *A Vacant Possession,* the first of several pamphlets that would solidify Fenton's reputation among poets before the broader acclaim of *The Memory of War.* (The chapbook or pamphlet has always been Fenton's true medium, and his poetic development is best measured by these smaller and more unified gatherings rather than the larger commercial volumes.) *A Vacant Possession* is noteworthy for helping to introduce a particular kind of narrative poem that quickly became popular among young poets—"the secret narrative." In the introduction to *Contemporary British Poetry* Morrison and Motion noted this self-consciously stylized type of narrative by saying, "We are often presented with stories that are incomplete, or are denied what might normally be considered essential information." The three narrative poems in this pamphlet—"A Vacant Possession," "Prison Island," and "Nest of Vampires"—were originally conceived by Fenton as part of a series called "Landscapes and Rooms" (to which the longer "A Staffordshire Murderer" also owes its origin). Each of these poems was to describe a particular landscape and interior via a different protagonist. The larger scheme was abandoned, but not before Fenton had written some striking poems.

"Nest of Vampires" is spoken by a young upper-class boy as his family packs up their belongings to move from their ancestral home. The child only vaguely realizes the financial ruin of his bickering family and the mismanagement of their estate, which has earned them the hatred of the villagers. Instead he imagines that his family suffers from some mysterious curse which he might unravel by finding the right clues. The poem plays with both the literary and the cinematic imagery of vampirism (garlic, mirrors, unspeakable family secrets, dogs whimpering for no reason). These gothic details not only project the child's guilty fears but also provide an implicit political metaphor for the class structure that permitted the landed family to destroy the villages around them.

These "secret narratives" are unfailingly interesting to read but ultimately unsatisfying to revisit. Stylish and self-assured, they create a brooding sense of atmosphere. At times they seem novelistic in their ability to present a welter of observed detail. Here is the opening of "A Vacant Possession":

> In a short time we shall have cleared the gazebo.
> Look how you can scrape the weeds from the paving stones
> With a single motion of the foot. Paths lead down
> Past formal lawns, orchards, notional guinea-fowl
> To where the house is entirely obscured from view.
>
> And there are gravel drives beneath the elm-tree walks
> On whose aquarium green the changing weather
> Casts no shadow. Urns pour their flowers out beside
> A weathered Atlas with the whole world to support.
> Look, it is now night and there are lights in the trees.
>
> The difficult guest is questioning his rival.
> He is pacing up and down while she leans against
> A mossy water-butt in which, could we see them,
> Innumerable forms of life are uncurving.
> She is bravely not being hurt by his manner
>
> Of which they have warned her. He taps his cigarette
> And brusquely changed the subject.

This is fine descriptive writing cast in sonorous twelve-syllable lines (a measure that usually seems flabby in English). Yet the poem never quite rises to the responsibilities of its own narrative. "A Vacant Possession" seems like a novella from which the plot has been excised. The characters never exist in meaningful relation to one another. The individual incidents do not coalesce into an integrated design. Even the subtext ultimately remains secret. Despite their masterful style, Fenton's "secret narratives" remain mostly pure atmosphere—poignant, evocative, but also evanescent. They display the author's considerable stylistic panache and originality, but they do not represent the work that makes Fenton's strongest claim on posterity. Those poems were still to come and very soon.

Toward the end of his journalistic stint in Germany, Fenton visited Vienna, where a friend was directing a play at the Burgtheater. The nerve-wracking excitement of the play's last-minute rehearsals made such an impression on Fenton that he decided to seek employment related to the theater. Returning to England in 1979, he eagerly filled the newly vacated post of theater critic for the *London Sunday Times.* This position not only inspired the lively reviews collected in *You Were Marvellous;* his turn toward literary journalism also provided the final impetus to get Fenton actively writing poetry again.

In 1980 *Quarto* published Fenton's poetic sequence "Elegy," which was based on the sketches he had begun in Berlin. Since English readers found the poem obscure, he revised and retitled it "A German Requiem" the next year, when his brother Tom printed the short sequence in a handsome folio for the newly established Salamander Press in Edinburgh. *A German Requiem* represented the first real breakthrough in establishing Fenton's poetic reputation. Andrew Motion praised it in the *New Statesman* (where Craig Raine had earlier praised *A Vacant Possession*), but, more important, Peter Porter, reviewing the book in the *Observer,* prophetically called Fenton "the most talented poet of his generation" and described the poem as "stately, composed, almost Eliotesque." The sequence also won the Southern Arts Literature Award for Poetry in 1981.

"A German Requiem" is an elegy for both the victims and the survivors of war. Based on Fenton's observations in Berlin and Urbino, the poem is an oblique narrative describing a visit to a German cemetery aboard "the Widow's Shuttle," a special bus, to attend a memorial service for the war dead and the painful meditations this excursion elicits. The poem progresses through a series of nine brief and fragmentary sections. The narrator seems to stand at a distance from the devastation he evokes. He never speaks in the first person but describes the participants as *you, they, he,* and *she.* (The only *I* in the poem is spoken by an unnamed man.) The narrator "deliberately chooses," as Andrew Motion has noted, "not to say certain things." Indeed, the particular style of the poem depends on the narrator reminding readers how much he chooses not to disclose—just as the poem's characters deliberately choose not to speak about certain parts of their wartime experiences.

Although cast as an elegy, the design of "A German Requiem" becomes clearer if the poem is read as a "secret narrative," perhaps Fenton's most fully realized poem in the genre. Like many of Fenton's early extended poems, "A German Requiem" can seem almost impenetrable unless the reader accepts the overt evasiveness of its narrator. A deliberately paradoxical poem, it evokes the memories of war without revealing them. From the first it insists that the clues to its own meaning are missing:

> It is not what they built. It is what they knocked down.
> It is not the houses. It is the spaces between the houses.
> It is not the streets that exist. It is the streets that no longer
>   exist.
> It is not your memories which haunt you.
> It is not what you have written down.
> It is what you have forgotten, what you must forget.

The necessity of forgetting is the central theme of "A German Requiem." While writing the poem, Fenton heard a psychologist lecture on the difficulty of defeated nations accommodating the memories of a lost war. Fenton linked this modern psychoanalytic idea to Thomas Hobbes's observation from *Leviathan* (1651), which serves as the epigraph to the poem, "Imagination and Memory are but one thing." The imaginative process of selectively recreating the past eventually becomes not only the survivors' tactic for living with the burden of history but also Fenton's aesthetic of writing political poetry. Although "A German Requiem" deals with a political subject, the poem avoids any specific political attachments or ideology (such as the international socialism to which the author then subscribed). Instead, Fenton seeks a broader consensus of common humanity. The poet is a concerned but objective witness to history. This carefully nonpartisan reportage also informs "Dead Soldiers," Fenton's most celebrated political poem, which was also published as a pamphlet in 1981.

"Dead Soldiers" describes an absurdly elegant battlefield

lunch Fenton the reporter had in 1973 with Prince Norodom Chantaraingsey, the military governor of Cambodia. Also present at the lunch is an obsequious, drunken aide who eventually proves to be the brother of Pol Pot, the revolutionary leader who will soon decimate Cambodia. The poem, which is both a journalistic account of this incident and a meditation on the impossibility of a foreigner's understanding the complexities of Cambodian politics, is narrated in a cool, factual style. Fenton's particular gift is to heighten the journalism into poetry by a series of quiet details—especially bitter puns and double entendres—seamlessly woven into the straightforward narrative. For example, the prince's expensive French brandy becomes a symbol for the decadence and inhumanity of the prince's regime:

> On every bottle, Napoleon Bonaparte
> Pleaded for the authenticity of the spirit.
> They called the empties Dead Soldiers
> And rejoiced to see them pile up at our feet.

In 1982 *The Memory of War* was published by Salamander Press to the most enthusiastic reception any young British poet had received since the appearance of Dylan Thomas. Almost immediately Fenton was hailed not only as one of the most accomplished poets of his generation but also as virtually unique, as Jonathan Raban stated in the *Sunday Times,* "in having a great deal to write about." Fenton's combination of technical skill and political insights appealed to a critical establishment that saw contemporary poetry as increasingly marginal in its relation to society. His political poetry was compared to the work of Auden, Yeats, Brodsky, and Akhamatova, and he was praised for bringing the prose virtues of clarity, accessibility, and directness successfully into poetry.

Fenton's immediate success was not altogether accidental, however much deserved. It also reflected the concerted efforts of the poet's supporters. Andrew Motion published a lengthy interview with Fenton in *Poetry Review* to coincide with the book's publication. (The issue even featured an earnest portrait of Fenton on its cover—wearing a bardic scowl worthy of John Milton.) *The Memory of War* was chosen as a Poetry Book Society

Recommendation before publication. Fenton's work also was featured prominently in Motion and Morrison's controversial but immensely influential *Penguin Book of Contemporary British Poetry*, which appeared within months of *The Memory of War*. This anthology announced a new generation of British poets which marked a decisive shift in sensibility and demanded, "for its appreciation, a reformation of poetic taste." These editorial claims were greatly overstated, since the poets included in the Penguin anthology did not cohere as a literary group in any meaningful sense, nor did the direction of their work appear particularly rebellious, as Auden and Larkin seemed to be their predominant influences. Nevertheless, these bold editorial gestures helped create an environment in which Fenton's quick rise to prominence was possible. And his new work was good enough to bear the weight of critical scrutiny.

Perhaps the most unexpected and oddly original success in *The Memory of War* is "The Skip," a remarkable narrative allegory. Like many of Fenton's best poems, this piece works through unusual combinations of form and content. The voice of the poem's persona, for example, is conversational and demotic, but it speaks in strictly rhymed heroic quatrains. Likewise this sustained allegory unfolds in a contemporary working-class neighborhood. Through these original juxtapositions Fenton creates a memorable comedy with the accessibility of a popular song and the integrity of a lyric poem. Telling the story of a cynical young man who literally throws his life away (*skip* is English slang for the large garbage containers Americans call *dumpsters*), the poem lightheartedly chronicles the narrator's despair and redemption in a casual manner closer to Kipling than to contemporary poetry.

> I took my life and threw it on the skip,
> Reckoning the next-door neighbours wouldn't mind
> If my life hitched a lift to the council tip
> With their dry rot and rubble. What you find
>
> With skips is—the whole community joins in.
> Old mattresses appear, doors kind of drift
> Along with all that won't fit in the bin
> And what the bin-men can't be fished to shift.

Amid the stark political poems and macabre secret narratives that make up the opening section of *The Memory of War,* "The Skip" seems oddly out of place. But it would prove a prophetic poem for Fenton. Its combination of comedy and violence, slangy diction and traditional meters, narrative form and symbolic intent, presages his later political satires like "Cut-Throat Christ" or "The Ballad of the Iman and the Shah." These poems astonishingly rehabilitate the populist mode of Kipling—used to very different political ends. They also demonstrate that Fenton's greatest originality is found not in his boldly experimental gestures like "Exempla" but in his highly individual combination of traditional elements to create unmistakably contemporary effects.

The Memory of War was followed in 1983 by *Children in Exile,* a short collection of eight poems of remarkable variety. The book opens with "Wind," one of Fenton's finest short lyrics. An apocalyptic poem, "Wind" counterpoints the timeless image of wind in a field of corn against the catastrophes of history.

> This is the wind, the wind in a field of corn.
> Great crowds are fleeing from a major disaster
> Down the long valleys, the green swaying wadis,
> Down through the beautiful catastrophe of wind.

"Wind" is followed by the sardonic "Lines for Translation into Any Language," an ingenious experimental piece which turns a numbered prose list into a powerful political poem. These poems deal with political subjects but in an unspecific, universalized way that helps prepare the reader for the delicate balance of the title poem, which tries to present the victims of a particular political upheaval with apolitical compassion.

"Children in Exile" is a discursive poem about contemporary politics that aspires to recreate in modern terms the familiar but dignified public style of eighteenth-century English verse. Written in a form invented by Fenton (a quatrain which alternates lines of free verse and rhymed pentameter), the poem is, according to the author, "a pastoral eclogue with political content," which owes its general conception to Thomas Gray's "Elegy Written in a Country Churchyard" (1751). The poem describes the painful but eventually successful transition of a family of four Cambodian refugees (a mother, two sons, and a daughter) who have escaped "the justice of Pol Pot" to live with a wealthy American family in northern Italy. Like the survivors in "A German Requiem," these refugees must learn to deal with the past which still haunts them in their dreams:

> They have found out: it is hard to escape from Cambodia,
>   Hard to escape the justice of Pol Pot,
> When they are called to report in dreams to their tormentors.
>   One night is merciful, the next is not.

One of Fenton's most refreshing accomplishments has been his nonsense verse. Almost half the work in his American selected volume, *Children in Exile: Poems 1968–1984,* is light or nonsense verse, including some of the best poems in the collection. Especially interesting has been his revival of the Audenesque genre of the apocalyptic nonsense poem. This genre typically starts in a brashly comic manner but slowly modulates into a nightmare vision, as in Fenton's "God, A Poem," which begins:

> A nasty surprise in a sandwich,
> A drawing-pin caught in your sock,
> The limpest of shakes from a hand which
> You'd thought would be firm as a rock,
>
> A serious mistake in a nightie,
> A grave disappointment all round
> Is all that you'll get from th'Almighty,
> Is all that you'll get underground.

The ironically playful treatment of serious themes gives Fenton's best nonsense verse the resonance of poetry in ways which could not be accomplished merely by ingenuity of language. Indeed a subtext of nihilism runs through his light verse. Even the titles of his nonsense poems, such as "This Octopus Exploits Women" or "The Killer Snails," often reveal a dark side to his imagination. In "The Song That Sounds Like This," a poem which like "A German Requiem" deliberately avoids stating its central theme, Fenton deals with depression and ennui (just as "The Skip" coyly plays with the themes of self-destruction and despair). Likewise in "The Wild Ones" Fenton turns gratuitous violence and sexual assault into farce by recreating a Grade-B motorcycle gang movie with a cast of South American rodents— coypus and capybaras. But even here the cartoon animal farce has an unexpected apocalyptic ending when the violated rodents give birth to freakish monsters:

> Months later, all the females have attacks
> And call the coypu doctors to their beds.
> What's born has dreadful capybara heads.

In 1983 a combined edition of *The Memory of War* and *Children in Exile* was published in England under the title of *Children in Exile: Poems 1968–1984* and appeared in America the next spring. This volume, which contained all of the poems that Fenton wished to preserve, solidified his reputation in the United Kingdom and earned him the most enthusiastic reception a young British poet has had in America for decades. In the *New Republic* Stephen Spender called Fenton "a brilliant poet of technical virtuosity," while Geoffrey Stokes in the *Village Voice* claimed his poems "aspire to greatness legitimately." In the *New York Review of Books* Seamus Heaney agreed that "Fenton's voice signals the emergence of a new poetic generation," while A. Poulin Jr. in the *New York Times Book Review* calmly reported that Fenton "already has all the earmarks of a genuinely major poet." *Newsweek* even listed Fenton as a possible successor to John Betjeman as Poet Laureate (which would ultimately be offered first to Philip Larkin and later accepted by Ted Hughes). Needless to say, *Children in Exile* was an amazing debut for a poet who had been unknown in America six months earlier.

While Fenton was not then a serious candidate for the Laureateship, he was at that time actively campaigning for an almost equally prestigious position, the Oxford Professorship of Poetry. Originally endowed in 1696, this professorship has had a distinguished list of occupants including Matthew Arnold, F. T. Palgrave, W. H. Auden, Robert Graves, and C. Day Lewis. Elected by a convocation of Oxford M.A.'s, the professorship, which carries a five-year term, provides the victor with only a meager salary but an influential public platform. At thirty-five Fenton was one of the youngest candidates in the professorship's history, but as an Oxford resident, he ran a popular campaign promising "to revive Auden's willingness to function as a campus poet." Ultimately Fenton lost the election to Peter Levi, another Oxford insider, but polled more votes than his distinguished elders Gavin Ewart and F. T. Prince. (He would eventually be elected to the professorship in 1994.) Fenton's disappointment, however, was undoubtedly softened by his receipt of the 1984 Geoffrey Faber Memorial Prize on the eve of the election.

Someday a biographer will tell us whether Fenton was downcast by his Oxford loss or cheered by the Faber Prize, but by now such small public victories or defeats hardly mattered in the real narrative of the poet's life. As an artist Fenton had already achieved something more noteworthy and enduring. By his mid-thirties he had emerged as the foremost English poet of his generation. (The professional literary critic in me wants to qualify that last statement by writing "one of the foremost English poets of his generation," but my conscience reminds me that there is no contemporary I would honestly rank above Fenton— at least without crossing the Irish sea.) The future would hold odd things for the poet. Circumstances would force him to leave England and revive his career in political journalism. His early contributions to the English version of the musical *Les Miserables* would unexpectedly make him wealthy and resettle him comfortably in Oxford. Opera translation and art criticism would play significant roles in his writing, and his later poetry would develop in ways both prefigured and unprecedented in his early work. Fenton would slowly become—how very English it seems to an American observer—a public institution. But all of that would now seem entirely appropriate because it was happening to a poet of true and durable distinction.

The Most Unfashionable Poet Alive

For half a century Charles Causley has stood apart from the mainstream of contemporary poetry. His work bears little relation to the most celebrated achievements of the Modernist movement but refers back to older, more specifically English roots. Taking his inspiration from folk songs, hymns, and especially ballads, Causley belongs—with A. E. Housman, Thomas Hardy, Rudyard Kipling, Walter de la Mare, Edward Thomas, Robert Graves, John Betjeman, Kingsley Amis, and Philip Larkin—to a conservative countertradition in English letters that stresses the fundamentally national character of its poetry and the essential role of popular forms in its inspiration.

Much of Causley's poetry has been written in the ballad form. Indeed, he is the most celebrated and accomplished living writer of ballads in English—an achievement many critics would consider less a distinction than a disability. His accomplishments, however, go far beyond the ballad; he has mastered an impressive variety of forms and styles. The true unity of his oeuvre depends less on a specific allegiance to any particular form than on his fundamental commitment to certain old-fashioned virtues of English poetry—simplicity, clarity, grace, and compassion. His work also demonstrates a conviction that the traditional forms of popular poetry remain living modes of expression, despite the Modernist revolution.

Causley has written accessibly in fixed forms in a period that prizes originality and unpredictability. He has endorsed the importance of narrative verse in an age which has called the very notion of poetic narrative into question. He has consistently addressed a common reader whom most critics maintain no

From the *Dark Horse* 5 (summer 1997): 22–27; 6 (spring 1998): 28–37.

longer exists. He has been a Christian poet in an agnostic age. He has even written poetry for children and placed some of it in his *Collected Poems* without qualification or apology. No wonder Causley goes unmentioned in critical literature. What words could adequately describe the magnificent indifference of the *au courant* to such as him—a homespun regionalist writing in discredited genres for an audience that has been declared extinct? To a serious critic, especially an American critic, Causley must seem in principle—for who, after all, would actually read him—the most unfashionable poet alive.

To call Causley's aesthetic conservative, however, fails to describe its radical independence from literary trends. He deserves some designation both more specific and more singular to differentiate him from fellow travelers of the counterrevolutionary fifties like Larkin and Amis. They made common cause of agnosticism in the face of international Modernism's Great Awakening. They share an intoxication with traditional meters (though all three write superbly in free verse when occasion demands). They recognize the efficiency of a clear narrative line, even in their lyrical utterances. Contrarians all, they came to maturity in the *Sturm und Drang* of Dylan Thomas and *The New Apocalypse*—a feverish milieu that confirmed their native anti-romanticism.

Not for working-class Causley, however, was the ironic detachment, emotional reserve, and guarded knowingness of his Oxonian counterparts. Causley possesses an essential innocence that Amis never reveals and Larkin hid under layers of ironic self-deprecation. Although their poetic tastes often coincide— and the three conspicuously share Hardy and Auden as decisive masters—their personalities differ dramatically. One sees the divergences most relevantly in their attitudes toward childhood. Amis seems never to have been a child; his life began with adolescence and its illicit pleasures of sex, liquor, tobacco, and literature. Larkin saw his own affluent but loveless boyhood as an unendurable emptiness. Causley's childhood, however, which was much harsher and more painful, often serves as a sacramental presence in his work. He presents no distinct adult persona—no cagey university librarian or sharp-clawed literary lion—separate from the Cornish schoolboy who has matured seamlessly into a successful writer. And yet, if Causley's innocence is tangible in the poetry, it has been tempered by hard experience of death, war, and suffering.

There is no better way to approach Causley's poetry than through his life, because few modern poets have been so meaningfully rooted in one time and place. Charles Stanley Causley was born in 1917 in the Cornish market town of Launceston where, except for six years of military service, he has lived ever since. Although he was too young to have any direct memories of the First World War, it profoundly shaped his childhood. His father, who had served as a private soldier in France, returned from the Great War a consumptive invalid. An only child, Causley spent his first seven years watching his father slowly die. He also watched the terrifying behavior of the shell-shocked soldiers who wandered through his native town. "From childhood, then," he remarked years later, "it had been made perfectly clear to me that war was something more than the exciting fiction one read about in books or saw on films."

From boyhood Causley intended to be an author. He began a novel at the age of nine and continued writing in a desultory fashion throughout his education at Launceston College. At fifteen, however, Causley quit school to begin working. He spent seven gloomy years first as a clerk in a builder's office and later working for a local electrical supply company. This period of isolation would have destroyed most aspiring young writers, but in Causley's case it proved decisive. Cut off from institutionalized intellectual life, he developed in the only way available—as an autodidact. "As far as poetry goes," Causley has commented on these formative years, "I'm self-educated. I read very randomly, I read absolutely everything." He also experimented—with poetry, fiction, and most successfully with drama. In the late thirties he published three one-act plays. During the same period Causley also played piano in a four-piece dance band, an experience which may have influenced his later predilection for writing poems in popular lyric forms such as the ballad.

In 1940 Causley joined the Royal Navy, in which he served for the next six years. Having spent all of his earlier life in tranquil Cornwall, he now saw wartime southern Europe, Africa, and Australia. Likewise, having already felt the tragedy of war through the early death of his father, Causley experienced it again more directly in the deaths of friends and comrades. These events decisively shaped his literary vision, pulling him from prose and drama into poetry. "I think I became a working poet the day I joined the destroyer *Eclipse* at Scapa Flow in August, 1940," he later wrote. "Though I wrote only fragmentary notes for the next three years, the wartime experience was a catalytic one. I knew that at last I had found my first subject, as well as a form." Although Causley wrote one book of short stories based on his years in the Royal Navy, *Hands to Dance* (1951; revised and enlarged in 1979 as *Hands to Dance and Skylark*), his major medium for portraying his wartime experiences has been poetry.

In August 1945 the Pacific war ended. (Causley witnessed the Japanese Southwest Pacific Command surrender on the flight deck of the aircraft carrier on which he was stationed.) Returning to Launceston, he entered the Peterborough Teacher's Training College to study English and history. Upon graduation he began teaching at the same grammar school in Launceston where he had studied as a boy. In 1951 Causley brought out his first collection, *Farewell, Aggie Weston,* a small pamphlet of thirty-one poems. A distillation of Causley's years in the navy, these early poems vividly re-create the alternately intoxicating and sobering experiences of a generation of young Englishmen who in fighting the Second World War discovered the wider world. Most of the poems depict the sailor's life in wartime, both on ship and in the strange port cities he visits on leave. In its colorful portrayal of navy life, *Farewell, Aggie Weston* remains one of the representative books of English poetry from the Second World War, and the poem "Chief Petty Officer" has become a definitive poem of the period, capturing a kind of naval character who typified the best and the worst of the British military traditions:

> He was probably made a Freemason in Hong Kong.
> He has a son (on War Work) in the Dockyard,
> And an appalling daughter
> In the WRNS.
> He writes on your draft-chit,
> Tobacco permit or request-form
> In a huge antique Borstal hand,
> . . . .

A whole war later
He will still be sitting under a pusser's clock
Waiting for tot-time,
His narrow forehead ruffled by the Jutland wind.

As the literary historian A. T. Tolley has noted, "Causley was one of the few poets to see the war continuously from the point of view of the lower ranks." *Farewell, Aggie Weston* also has documentary importance since the poems incorporate a wealth of traditional and contemporary naval slang (much of which Causley explains in footnotes). Like Kipling fifty years earlier, Causley demonstrated that the best way to capture the true character of military men was to use their special language. This small volume provides a unique poetic record of the British navy in its last moment of imperial self-confidence.

Although *Farewell, Aggie Weston* is not Causley's best book, it already reveals a poet with an unusual voice and perspective. It also foreshadows the themes and techniques of his later work. Writing in both free and formal verse, Causley uses each technique in particular ways to which he returns repeatedly in his subsequent career. His free verse is loose, cadenced speech used mainly for carefully detailed descriptive poems, whereas his metered verse, cast mainly in rhymed quatrains, is used mostly for narrative and dramatic poems. Not surprisingly, given Causley's later eminence as a master of traditional forms, the best poems in *Farewell, Aggie Weston* are in rhyme and meter, usually in ballad stanzas, such as his memorable "Nursery Rhyme of Innocence and Experience."

Written at the height of British Neo-romanticism, which made personal style and individual voice the preconditions of artistic authenticity, Causley's "Nursery Rhyme of Innocence and Experience" revels in its impersonality. The poem is anonymous in the sense of the finest traditional ballads—the author's individuality has defiantly appropriated a universal style. If Blake chose the term *song* in his "Songs of Innocence and Experience" to denote their radical simplicity and directness of expression versus conventional eighteenth-century literary "poems," then Causley's title suggests his deliberate attempt to recapture a straightforward Blakean clarity. The poem concludes with this exchange between a returning sailor and the boy to whom he has bought gifts:

> "*O are you the boy*
>   *Who would wait on the quay*
> *With the silver penny*
>   *And the apricot tree?*
>
> "*I've a plum-coloured fez*
>   *And a drum for thee*
> *And a sword and a parakeet*
>   *From over the sea.*"
>
> "O where is the sailor
>   With bold red hair?
> And what is that volley
>   On the bright air?
>
> "O where are the other
>   Girls and boys?
> And why have you brought me
>   Children's toys?"

Thematically, *Farewell, Aggie Weston* presents the issues that would concern Causley throughout his career—the harsh reality of war ("Son of the Dying Gunner"), the tragic deaths of the young and promising ("A Ballad for Katharine of Aragon"), the fascination of foreign landscapes ("HMS *Glory* at Sydney"), and, most important, the fall from innocence to experience, a sense of which pervades the entire volume. Only Causley's restless, visionary Christianity is specifically absent from the volume, although with the gift of hindsight one can see the elements which nurtured it in several of the poems about death and war.

Although Causley's second volume, *Survivor's Leave* (1953), does not mark a broadening of his poetic concerns, it demonstrates a liberating concentration of their treatment. Abandoning cadenced free verse and the documentary aesthetic it embodied for him, Causley perfected the tightly formal poems for which he would become best known. All of the poems in *Survivor's Leave* are written in rhyme and meter, a common coin which he now uses in a distinctive way. His rhythms move with deliberate regularity, and the diction has a timeless traditional quality—often consciously "timeless" in Causley's growing tendency to scrub language clean of specific period references. His full rhymes chime boisterously at the end of each line. Sometimes deliberately unsophisticated, these poems often emulate the texture of folk poetry or popular song, which gives them an unusual openness and immediacy. In an age when sophisticated poets writing in rhyme and meter often try to disguise or underplay the acoustic patterns of their verse, Causley is a radical traditionalist, a cunning voluntary primitive, who takes unabashed delight in the joyful noise his forms make.

Survivor's Leave also specifically demonstrates Causley's growing mastery of the ballad and contains two of his finest poems in that form, "Recruiting Drive" and "Ballad of the Faithless Wife." These poems both show the influence of W. H. Auden, whose work initially provided Causley with a model of how to rejuvenate the traditional form with bold metaphors, slangy diction, and unapologetic symbolism. Causley's often anthologized poem "On Seeing a Poet of the First World War at the Station of Abbeville" (a composite portrait based on Edmund Blunden, Siegfried Sasson, and the poet's father) also incorporates techniques from Auden's lyric poetry (even as its title echoes Betjeman's "On Seeing an Old Poet in the Café Royal"). Although Causley learned much from Auden, his work never feels derivative. Causley's tone is less knowing and more vulnerable, his range of allusion less cosmopolitan, his presentation more unabashedly narrative and less overtly analytic.

As the book's title suggests, Causley's major theme in *Survivor's Leave* once again is war, though here the conflict has been universalized beyond the Second World War into a tragic view of life as a doomed struggle between the evil and the innocent. The book bristles with images of violence and deception. In "Recruiting Drive" a butcher-bird lures young men to their deaths in battle. (A few months after the appearance of *Survivor's Leave*, Auden first published a similar poem, "The Willow-wren and the Stare," in *Encounter*. Perhaps Causley had some slight influence on his own mentor.)

Under the willow the willow
　　I heard the butcher-bird sing,
Come out you fine young fellow
*　　From under your mother's wing.*
I'll show you the magic garden
*　　That hangs in the beamy air,*
The way of the lynx and the angry Sphinx
*　　And the fun of the freezing fair.*

Lie down lie down with my daughter
*　　Beneath the Arabian tree,*
Gaze on your face in the water
*　　Forget the scribbling sea.*
Your pillow the nine bright shiners
*　　Your bed the spilling sand,*
But the terrible toy of my lily-white boy
*　　Is the gun in his innocent hand.*

In "Cowboy Song" another young man, bereft of family, knows he will be murdered before his next birthday. Even a seemingly straightforward narrative such as the "Ballad of the Faithless Wife" acquires a dark visionary quality when, in the last stanza, personal tragedy unexpectedly modulates into allegory:

False O false was my lover
　　Dead on the diamond shore
White as a fleece, for her name was Peace
　　And the soldier's name was War.

Causley's vision in *Survivor's Leave* is so bleak that he even rejects God's role as guardian and savior of humanity. In "I Saw a Shot-down Angel," for example, a wounded Christ figure crudely rebuffs the compassionate narrator's attempts to help him, thereby denying the redemptive nature of his suffering:

My angel spat my solace in my face
And fired my fingers with his burning shawl,
Crawling in blood and silver to a place
Where he could turn his torture to the wall.

Union Street (1957) secured Causley's reputation as an important contemporary poet. Published with a preface by Edith

Sitwell, then at the height of her influence, *Union Street* collected the best poems from Causley's first two volumes and added nineteen new ones, including two of his finest poems ever, "I Am the Great Sun" and "At the British War Cemetery, Bayeux," the last of which Sitwell singled out for particular praise. In her preface Sitwell placed Causley's work in its proper historical perspective—English folk song and ballad. While Sitwell praised Causley's traditional roots, she also noted his "strange individuality." Like most of Causley's admirers, however, Sitwell had difficulty in explaining the particular appeal of his work. To express her approval, she repeatedly resorted to vague exclamations of delight, such as "beautiful," "deeply moving," and "enchanting." While these terms describe in some general way the effect Causley's poetry has on a sympathetic reader, they are so subjective that they shed little light on the special nature of his literary achievement. Unfortunately, Sitwell's response typifies Causley's critical reception. His admirers have felt more comfortable in writing appreciations of his work than in examining it in critical terms. The truly "strange individuality" that makes Causley a significant and original artist rather than a *faux-naif* has never been adequately explained. This situation has given most critics the understandable but mistaken impression that while Causley's poetry may be enjoyed, it is too simple to bear serious analysis.

The "strange individuality" of Causley's style is easily observed, but only with some difficulty can it be discussed without fatal simplification. It will hardly help to say that his style explores the illuminating contrasts between the familiar and the unexpected. That contrast, after all, is a general principle of most art (and certainly all formal poetry). It is, however, useful to note that few poets have pushed this principle to such an extreme—or at least have *successfully* negotiated that extreme. For him contrast and disjunction have become not only a stylistic device but an organizing principle and thematic obsession. One finds the principle in both the microcosm and the macrocosm of Causley's poetry. His diction, for instance, characteristically combines the ordinary and the odd. Notice the strange adjectives used to modify otherwise conventional images ("Forget the *scribbling* sea" or "write with *loud* light / the *mineral* air"). Framed in the regular meters, linear narrative, and otherwise accessible style of the traditional ballad, the disjunctive moments acquire a mysteriously heightened effect that they would not possess in, say, a Surrealist poem where synesthesia, discontinuity, free association, and non-naturalistic description are expected. The disjunctions that characterize Causley's poetry are, of course, neither so prolific or extreme as the Surrealist method. His poems usually contrast two different types of diction, tone, imagery, and even narrative outcome—the domestic and military, the mundane and transcendent, the private and public, the formal and slangy, and, in his religious verse, the sacred and profane. The poem is almost always rooted in one world. The narrative unfolds from a familiar base in what should be a conventional manner, but the second world then unpredictably interpenetrates the fabric of the poem. The strange frisson of Causley's best poetry, that elusive quality that Sitwell and others have registered, arises out of this disjunction, which often feels involuntary or unconscious on the part of the author—an innocent, visionary quality reminiscent of Blake.

Compare these two stanzas from Blake's "London" with the opening of Causley's "At the British War Cemetery, Bayeux":

> I wander thro' each charter'd street
> Near where the charter'd Thames does flow,
> And mark in every face I meet
> Marks of weakness, marks of woe.
> . . . .
> How the chimney-sweeper's cry
> Every black'ning church appalls;
> And the hapless soldier's sigh
> Runs in blood down palace walls.
>
> —Blake

> I walked where in their talking graves
> And shirts of earth five thousand lay,
> When history with ten feasts of fire
> Had eaten the red air away.
>
> —Causley

The resemblance is not merely a matter of rhyme and meter, stanza and tone. It is also one of spiritual genealogy—of primal sympathy and imaginative temperament. Like the Blake of *Songs of Innocence and of Experience,* Causley is a demotic visionary, a poet who finds the divine—and the demonic—in the everyday world and reports it without apology in the available forms and accessible images of his time and place. Causley's characteristic mode is often the short narrative (and he has never been tempted into the epic private mythology of the late Prophetic Books), but his decisive source is not Hardy or Auden, as important as they were in other ways, but Blake. His late eighteenth-century master, moreover, also provided him a potent example of how the poetic outsider can become a seer—a lesson not likely to be lost on a working-class Cornish writer remote from the Oxbridge world of literary London forty years ago.

The visionary mode has its greatest range of expression in Causley's religious poetry. No reader of *Farewell, Aggie Weston* would have guessed that its author would become one of the few contemporary Christian poets of genuine distinction. Yet the new poems in *Union Street* confirmed Causley's transformation from veteran to visionary. The devotional sonnet "I Am the Great Sun," which opens the section of new poems, reveals a more overtly compassionate side to Christianity than found in *Survivor's Leave.* Here Christ speaking from the cross (the poem was inspired by a seventeenth-century Norman crucifix) announces his doomed love for man:

> I am the great sun, but you do not see me,
>   I am your husband, but you turn away.
> I am the captive, but you do not free me,
>   I am the captain you will not obey.
>
> I am the truth, but you will not believe me,
>   I am the city where you will not stay,
> I am your wife, your child, but you will leave me,
>   I am that God to whom you will not pray.

This poem reverses the worldview of "I Saw a Shot-down Angel," where man shows compassion for the suffering Christ figure. Here Christ tries to guide and protect humanity, but mankind refuses to acknowledge him: and yet the sonnet presents some hope. Although man lives in an evil world, salvation is at least offered.

The other new poems in *Union Street* reflect this glimmer of hope without obscuring the bitter realism of Causley's earlier work. In "At the British War Cemetery, Bayeux," for example, the grief-stricken narrator walks among the graves of the slain soldiers and asks them what gift he can offer beyond his tears. They reply that, since he cannot restore them to life, he should use their deaths as an inspiration to live more fully.

> *Take,* they replied, *the oak and laurel.*
> *Take our fortune of tears and live*
> *Like a spendthrift lover. All we ask*
> *Is the one gift you cannot give.*

Love in its broadest Christian sense has become for Causley the means to redemption, but the poet has no illusions that redemption will prove easy. Only one character in *Union Street* actually achieves salvation through love—Sir Henry Trecarell, a sixteenth-century Cornish lord, who survives the sorrow of his son's death by devoting his wealth to rebuilding the local church at the request of St. Mary Magdalene. Most of Causley's characters, however, lack the strength and wealth of Trecarell, and no saints intervene miraculously to guide them. They are tantalized by the notion of redemption but unable to achieve it.

Causley's next volume, *Johnny Alleluia* (1961), continues to explore the visionary possibilities of the demotic style. This fourth collection presents no stylistic break with *Survivor's Leave* or *Union Street*. The poems remain exclusively in rhyme and meter, though Causley uses traditional prosodic forms with more overt sophistication to deal with increasingly complex material. The ballad continues to be his central form, though one now notices a pronounced division in the kinds of ballads Causley writes. In addition to ballads on contemporary themes (whose effects are often primarily lyrical), each volume now contains a group of strictly narrative ballads usually based on historical or legendary Cornish subjects. While Causley had from the beginning experimented with recreating the folk ballad, this enterprise now becomes a major preoccupation. In the introduction to his anthology *Modern Ballads and Story Poems* (1965), Causley confesses the basis of his fascination with "the ancient virtues of this particular kind of writing." The narrative poem or ballad, he writes, allows the poet to speak "without bias or sentimentality." It keeps the author from moralizing, but it "allows the incidents of his story to speak for themselves, and, as we listen, we remain watchful for all kinds of ironic understatements."

Johnny Alleluia also marks a deepening of Causley's thematic concerns. Many poems explore his complex vision of Christ as humanity's redeemer. Fully half the poems in this volume use Christ figures either explicitly, as in "*Cristo de Bristol*" and "Emblems of the Passion," or by implication, in strange transformations such as those in "For an Ex–Far East Prisoner of War" and "Guy Fawkes' Day," where the effigy burning in the holiday fire becomes a redemptive sacrificial victim. Likewise Causley alternates scurrilous parodies of the Christ story, such as "Sonnet to the Holy Vine" and the more disturbing "Master and Pupil," with his most devout meditations. Reading his many treatments of the Christian drama, one sees that Causley believes in the redemptive nature of Christ's sacrifice, but that he doubts man's ability to accept Christ's love without betraying it.

Johnny Alleluia is also Causley's first volume that does not deal specifically with the War. While his concerns remain basically the same, they are now reflected in civilian themes, especially in such vignettes of urban delinquents as "My Friend Maloney" and "Johnny Alleluia." Only once does World War II literally come to haunt the present—in "Mother, Get Up, Unbar the Door," where a woman's lover, killed nearly twenty years before at Alamein, returns from the grave to claim her daughter in a ghostly union. Here Causley shows remarkable skill at transposing a traditional ghost ballad into convincing contemporary terms. Causley also pursues his concern with the fall from innocence in "Healing a Lunatic Boy," possibly his most vivid presentation of this central theme. Here a lunatic boy, who originally experiences the world in a direct way reminiscent of Adam's in the Garden of Eden, is brought back to a mundane sense of reality by his cure. Causley contrasts the brilliant and metaphorical world of madness with the prosaic and literal world of sanity:

Trees turned and talked to me,
    Tigers sang,
Houses put on leaves,
    Water rang.
Flew in, flew out
    On my tongue's thread
A speech of birds
    From my hurt head.
. . . .
Now river is river
    And tree is tree,
My house stands still
    As the northern sea.
On my hundred of parables
    I heard him pray,
Seize my smashed world,
    Wrap it away.

In *Underneath the Water* (1968), Causley's most personal book of poems, he speaks frankly of both his childhood and adulthood. The poems about his boyhood are especially important in understanding his work. Although he had written a great deal about childhood earlier in his career, until his fifth collection of poems he rarely discussed his own. The childhood poems in *Underneath the Water,* therefore, illuminate the personal background of his most central themes. The volume opens with "By St. Thomas Water," Causley's most complex view of the fall from innocence to experience. Two children (one of them seemingly a version of the author), looking for a jar to fish with, steal one holding withered flowers on a tombstone. Before they go, they playfully decide to listen for the dead man's voice in the grave. Much to their horror, they think they hear him murmuring indistinctly underground. Noticing the tombstone's legend, "He is not dead but sleeping," they flee in terror. The narrator then spends the rest of his life wondering what the dead man tried to tell him.

In this volume Causley also gives several views of himself as an adult, especially as a teacher of the young—a vocation he finds problematic and even at times frightening in poems such as "School at Four O'Clock" and "Conducting a Children's

Choir." But the most disturbing view of his adult life comes in "Trusham," in which he revisits the village where his father and grandfather were born. He reads his dead father's name on the local war memorial, and even meets an old family acquaintance, who rebukes him for failing to carry on the family name by marrying. These experiences set off a crisis in the poet's mind which ends in a vision of his own cold and barren future.

In his first five volumes—from *Farewell, Aggie Weston* to *Underneath the Water*—Causley may have appeared unconcerned with literary trends but not necessarily contrarian or reactionary. His aesthetic posture seemed not only natural but almost inevitable since he displayed such an easy and authentic link to older traditions. With the publication of *Figure of 8* (1969), however, the contrarian Causley emerges. It would be hard to overstate how uniquely odd this volume seems compared to the influential poets of the late sixties and early seventies. Free verse and the lyric mode had become *de rigueur* even in England, and bitterly confessional poetry was in full vogue. Robert Lowell, Sylvia Plath, John Berryman, and the Beats had reached the height of their influence. It was the era of *Crow, The Maximus Poems, The Lice,* and *Ariel.* Serious poets were expected to "grow"—that is, change their styles in accordance with the times. For formal poets, like Donald Hall, James Wright, Donald Davie, and Anne Stevenson, "growth" inevitably meant exploring free verse. In such a milieu *Figure of 8,* a collection of eight, mostly lengthy rhymed narratives, stands as Causley's one ostentatiously reactionary volume. Not only did it flaunt fashion by offering long, impersonal stories in rocking rhyme and meter; it broke a primal taboo of contemporary literature by offering the same poems to a mixed audience of children and adults.

Causley has stated iconoclastically that "the only difference between an adult poem and a children's poem is the *range* of the audience." A children's poem "is a poem that has to work for the adult and the child as well." Cogent though it may be, Causley's aesthetic hardly reflects mainstream literary opinion, which relegates children's poetry to subliterary status—even lower, if such a Stygian level exists, than that of rhymed narrative poetry. *Figure of 8* is Causley's most contrarian volume not only in form but also in content. All but one of his poems eschew contemporary subjects for those of traditional balladry (Bible stories, legends of the saints, war tales). The poems' tone and diction remain stylized, and although written with consummate skill, they imitate traditional folk balladry so closely that they border on pastiche and too often betray the predictability and tameness of imitative writing. However enjoyable, the poems lack the quirky resonance and psychological depth—that "strange individuality"—of Causley's best writing.

These historical ballads seem to have answered a deep need in Causley's imagination for impersonal, public subject matter. If one compares his early work with that of his contemporaries, one notices immediately how seldom he wrote overt autobiography. The subjects (like the Navy) or locations (like Gibraltar) might be openly drawn from the poet's personal experience, but their treatment almost always reflects some conscious objectification. Causley's first published works were plays, and his early poetry displays a dramatist's instinct for the expressive possibilities of impersonality. The poems may speak in the first person, but the *I* is almost always a fictive character. World War II had initially provided him with accessible public subjects, but as he exhausted that material, he moved increasingly back into Cornish history. Like the war, local history grew naturally out of his personal experience, and it invited impersonal narrative treatment.

If Causley's loyalty to the ballad form appears a conspicuous anachronism, so, too, does his reliance on public subjects, historical material, and the narrative mode. He has been in almost every sense an outsider to the mainstream of contemporary poetry. His historical ballads in particular not only reject the metrical conventions of midcentury poetry (a tuneful stanza too simple for sophisticated formalists and too traditional for progressives); they also reject the notion that a poet creates a private reality in the context of his or her own poems. No private mythologies now for Causley. His work makes its appeal to a common reality outside the poem—usually an objectively verifiable reality of history or geography. Causley's public is no ideological abstraction; his ideal readers are local and concrete—the Cornish. His regionalism grows naturally out of his aesthetic. The public nature of this imaginative gesture is also reinforced by Causley's habitual measure, the ballad, the most popular and accessible form in English.

Seen from this perspective, even Causley's often idiosyncratic religious poems take on a public aspect since they grow out of the shared Christian faith of Cornwall. If the bizarre turns of "Bible Story," *"Cristo de Bristol,"* and "I Saw a Shot-down Angel" seem distinctly unorthodox in their treatment of the Christian mythos, that is a traditional freedom of the regional artist. Being so deeply rooted in one place and culture allows a genuine writer to experiment wildly with the material without ever losing touch with its essence. Causley's religious poems recall the work of another regional writer, Flannery O'Connor, who also understood the transfiguring violence at the center of Christian redemption. Religion is not literary subject matter to either writer; it is part of the daily texture of their lives in a specific time and place. If Causley's religious poems often unfold like private visions, those visions grow recognizably from a common, public mythos. If they often present images and situations which seem extravagant or oddly proportioned, these poems are not so much surreal as primitive and symbolic in their method—in much the same way that an early Renaissance painting might present a blue-robed Madonna holding a diminutive moon or a castle in her hand and standing in a strange, unearthly landscape. While such art may not be realistic in a strict sense, it deals intelligibly with a widely understood set of symbols.

Causley is one of today's preeminent writers of children's poetry, and his children's verse bears an illuminating relation to his work for adults. "When I write a poem," Causley has commented, "I don't know whether it's for a child or adult." His children's book *Figgie Hobbin* (1970), for instance, reveals the continuity of his work. Although the poems in *Figgie Hobbin* are simple in structure and often written from a child's perspective, they are almost indistinguishable from his adult verse. (It is instructive to remember that Blake published his *Songs of Innocence* as an illustrated children's book. It was posterity that reclassified it to the more respectable category of pure lyric.) In these children's poems he explores his major themes in a fully characteristic way. Indeed they fit seamlessly into the *Collected Poems* (1975), where they are presented without comment among his adult poems. Moreover, as a group, these tight and polished poems rank high among Causley's published work, and validate his theory that a truly successful children's poem is also a genuine adult poem. "What Has Happened to Lulu?," "Tell Me, Tell Me, Sarah Jane," and "If You Should Go to Caistor Town" are among Causley's most accomplished ballads; "I Saw a Jolly Hunter" is among his best humorous poems. "I Am the Song" has an epigrammatic perfection that eludes classification, and "Who?" may be the finest lyric he has ever written.

The simplicity of the poems in *Figgie Hobbin* reveals his method more clearly. Their clarity and grace epitomize the transparent style that he has striven for throughout his career. As he has reminded readers, "The mere fact of a poem appearing simple in language and construction bears no relation whatsoever to the profundity of ideas it may contain." The meaning of many apparently simple poems is rich and complex, just as the underlying meaning of an overtly difficult poem may be crude and banal. The direct and uncomplicated voice that speaks in Causley's children's verse is traditional in the most radical sense. Causley has so thoroughly assimilated certain traditions of English verse that he uses them naturally to translate personal experiences into a common utterance. There is no gap between the demands of private sensibility and the resources of a public style. His work achieves the lucid impersonality of folk song or ballad. In "Who?," for example, Causley's vision of his lost childhood remains equally authentic on either a personal or universal level:

> Who is that child I see wandering, wandering
> Down by the side of the quivering stream?
> Why does he seem not to hear, though I call to him?
> Where does he come from, and what is his name?
> . . . .
> Why does he move like a wraith by the water,
> Soft as the thistledown on the breeze blown?
> When I draw near him so that I may hear him,
> Why does he say that his name is my own?

Causley's unabashed traditionalism has left him open to attack from critics. Christopher Ricks, for example, has dismissed

Causley's commitment to revive the ballad as a quixotic pursuit of an almost impossible ideal. Writing in the *New York Times Book Review*, Ricks declared that Causley's poetry "embarks upon a task which is beyond its talents true though those are, since it is beyond talent: to tap again the age-old sources which have become clogged, cracked, buried. . . . It would take genius to recreate the world, as something other than a recreation. Causley has much talent and no genius." There is much truth in Ricks's assumption; skill alone cannot revive a dead literary form. While Ricks's criticism may describe the dilute nature of Causley's most narrowly derivative work—the archaically stylized ballads on traditional themes—it does not adequately account for the persuasive authenticity of his finest poems. Causley's oeuvre is too diverse to be so narrowly characterized. As for *genius*, it is a word not to be used lightly. But if poems like "At the British War Cemetery, Bayeux," "I Am the Great Sun," "Recruiting Drive," "Innocent's Song," and "Who?" show only *talent,* then talent is a far rarer commodity in contemporary poetry than generally assumed.

Collected Poems (1975) solidified Causley's reputation in England and broadened his audience in America. The volume was widely reviewed on both sides of the Atlantic almost entirely in a positive light, but most critics presented Causley's achievement in a reductive manner. While they admired the ease and openness of his work and praised his old-fashioned commitment to narrative poetry, they did not generally find the resonance of language that distinguishes the finest contemporary poetry. By implication, therefore, they classified Causley as an accomplished minor poet, an engagingly eccentric antimodernist, who had mastered the traditional ballad at the expense of more experimental work. Only Edward Levy's essay on the *Collected Poems* in Manchester's *PN Review* made a serious attempt to demonstrate the diversity of Causley's achievement and his importance as a lyric poet. Fortunately, subsequent critics such as Robert McDowell, D. M. Thomas, Michael Schmidt, and Samuel Maio have followed Levy's lead to make broader claims for Causley's work.

Most critics also missed the unexpected direction signaled by the twenty-three new poems in the collection. While continuing to employ rhyme and meter, Causley returned to free verse for the first time since *Farewell, Aggie Weston*. This shift opened his work to new effects while liberating his talent for description. In "Ten Types of Hospital Visitor," which opens the "New Poems" section of his *Collected Poems*, Causley creates a detailed panorama of hospital life which unexpectedly modulates from realism to visionary fancy. In "Ward 14" Causley uses free verse to achieve painful directness in his description of a man visiting his old, brain-damaged mother in the hospital. These poems demonstrate a richness of depiction and high degree of psychological naturalism not often found in Causley's earlier work. They also reveal the increasingly autobiographic interests that would characterize his later work. While mastering new techniques, however, Causley did not jettison traditional form. He ends the *Collected Poems* with several formal poems, most notably "A Wedding Portrait," one of his most important poems of self-definition. Here the poet's past and present, innocence and experience, are literally embodied in the scene of his middle-aged self looking at his parents' wedding photograph. His doomed father and mother appear innocently hopeful in the portrait while the adult poet knows the subsequent pain they will undergo. His present knowledge cannot help them escape their plight, and he remains cut off from them now by time and death as absolutely as he was nonexistent to them on their wedding day. In a visionary moment Causley looks to his art to bridge the gap in time and restore his dead parents to him and his lost childhood self to them. The 1975 *Collected Poems* ends with the affirmation of poetry's power to triumph over death:

> I am a child again, and move
> Sunwards these images of clay,
> Listening for their first birth-cry.
> And with the breath my parents gave
> I warm the cold words with my day:
> Will the dead weight to fly. To fly.

Causley's later work has continued to show remarkable range and development. The older Causley has not merely changed but grown: he has explored new modes of expression without losing mastery over the forms at which he earlier excelled. The section of new poems that concludes the 1992 British *Collected Poems* (or the American edition of *Secret Destinations* in 1989) shows an impressive diversity of forms, genres, and styles. Autobiographical lyrics like "Eden Rock" and children's poems like "I Am the Song" meet on equal terms with narrative ballads, war poems, free verse travelogues, religious meditations, and translations. No single style predominates, and all are handled with assurance. Few poets in their seventh and eight decades have written so much or so consistently well. Changes in his life may have helped broaden Causley's perspective. Retiring from full-time teaching in 1976, for the first time he devoted himself entirely to writing. His international reputation also earned him opportunities to travel abroad. Just as his wartime travel provided poetic inspiration, these recent journeys have spurred him to unexpected work. While still writing about his native Cornwall in such characteristic poems as "Seven Houses" and "On Launceston Castle," he has turned his attention to foreign landscapes, especially Australia. He has also sharpened his gift for psychological portraiture in poems such as "Grandmother," which describes a wise and resilient old German woman who has survived the Second World War.

Now eighty, Charles Causley stands as one of Britain's three or four finest living poets. He is the master of at least five major poetic modes or genres—the short narrative, the war poem, the religious poem, children's poetry, and the personal lyric. The historical accident that none of these categories, except the last, is currently fashionable among literary critics will not concern posterity. Nor does it greatly concern most contemporary readers. No other living British poet of Causley's distinction rivals his general popularity or commands so diverse a readership. His admirers stretch from schoolchildren to his fellow poets. (After Betjeman's death, British poets voted Causley as their first choice to become the next Poet Laureate.) The special quality of this esteem is evident in the comments of the current Laureate, Ted Hughes:

> Among the English poetry of the last half century, Charles Causley's could well turn out to be the best loved and most

needed. . . . Before I was made Poet Laureate, I was asked to name my choice of the best poet for the job. Without hesitation I named Charles Causley—this marvellously resourceful, original poet, yet among all known poets the only one who could be called a man of the people, in the old, best sense. A poet for whom the title might have been invented afresh. I was pleased to hear that in an unpublished letter Philip Larkin thought the same and chose him too.

Best Loved. Most needed. Man of the people. These are not phrases one is accustomed to hear concerning a contemporary poet. Surely some readers find them embarrassing. Add to this list Sitwell's compliment that "these poems are among the natural growths of our soil, like our sweet and exquisite folk-songs, and our strange ballads." Is there a literary theorist listening who isn't by now reaching for his or her revolver? To be consummately offensive to what James Fenton called "ghastly good taste," why not quote some rhymed compliments? In one of his last published poems, Philip Larkin wrote:

> Ah, CHARLES, be reassured! For you
> Make lasting friends with all you do,
> And all you write; your truth and sense
> We count on as a sure defense
> Against the trendy and the mad
> The feeble and the downright bad.

Truth. Sense. One hopes by now everyone has found something at which to cringe. These are not respectable terms to describe—let alone praise—serious poetry at the end of the twentieth century. But what if Hughes, Sitwell, and Larkin are right in the criteria they use? Not right for every poet in every period but for the particular case of Causley? What if he is indeed a poet who has found an authentic, inventive, and powerful way to do what poets have traditionally done—give their own people unforgettable and truthful words, images, and stories by which to apprehend their lives and time? Some readers think so. Count me as one of them.

Home Is So Sad

Philip Larkin was the great poet no one expected. In an age of progressive politics, experimental art, and cosmopolitan culture, this flabby, bald, bespectacled bachelor librarian seemed to inhabit a world untouched by intellectual fashions. Socially reactionary, poetically conservative, and defiantly provincial, he wrote against the mainstream poetry of his age and gradually refashioned it in his own eccentric image.

When Larkin died in 1985 at the age of sixty-three, the reclusive poet was a national figure in England. His fame had the paradoxical quality on which great reputations are made. Because he avoided the press, it adored him. (He refused, for example, to be the subject of a television documentary for years until the producers paid him two thousand pounds and did not require him to appear on camera.) Because he declined to give public readings, others performed his work in one-man shows, cabaret productions, and literary events like "An Evening Without Philip Larkin." In 1984 he was offered the Poet Laureateship, but, to the disappointment of both Margaret Thatcher and the media, he declined. "I dream of becoming Laureate," he told the press, "and wake up screaming." His final illness was national news. Although he had published virtually no poetry for a decade (except his chilling vision of death, "Aubade"), his obituaries did not hesitate to label him "the greatest living poet in our language." Even the Communist *Morning Star* ran the headline "Best-Selling Poet Dies in Private Hospital." No British poet since Tennyson had simultaneously captivated both the

Published as "The Still, Sad Music of Philip Larkin," review of *Philip Larkin: A Writer's Life,* by Andrew Motion, from the *Washington Post Book World,* August 15, 1993, 1.

literati and the common reader. He was the only living poet many of them knew by heart.

After Larkin's death his reputation continued to rise, both in England and abroad. He now stands securely with Thomas Hardy, William Butler Yeats, and W. H. Auden as one of the century's four indisputably great poets born in the British Isles. Next to the voluminous works of his prolific companions, however, Larkin's legacy looks weirdly parsimonious. His claims to posterity rest mainly on three proverbially thin volumes of verse—*The Less Deceived* (1955), *The Whitsun Weddings* (1964), and *High Windows* (1974)—and a few posthumously collected late poems. This core oeuvre consists of around ninety poems, few of them longer than a page. How did Larkin get so far on so little? By a rare combination of imaginative and critical genius. Every poem in his mature collections is genuinely interesting, and at least two dozen of them rank among the best English-language poems of the century.

Last year, however, a major scandal erupted in England with the publication of Larkin's letters. Probably the most consistently smutty correspondence ever produced by a major poet, his private missives bristle with racist remarks, misogynistic sneers, crude sexuality, and personal invective. Larkin's celebrated sense of humor is almost everywhere apparent, but it cannot hide his extraordinary solipsism, petty rages, and whining self-pity. Critics quickly lambasted Larkin's sexism and racism, but I doubt that it was the poet's politically incorrect attitudes that so deeply unsettled his admirers. Larkin's xenophobia, misogamy, and reactionism had long been legendary. What truly shocked people was the sheer crudity of his prejudice, the cruelty of his self-absorption, and his gross insensitivity to the people who loved him most. How could this smug, irritable voice have spoken so many of the tenderest and saddest poems in the language?

Andrew Motion's new biography, *Philip Larkin: A Writer's Life*, sets about exploring that paradox with admirable intelligence and candor. Motion brings four considerable advantages to his complex undertaking. First, he is an accomplished poet who understands Larkin's cultural milieu from the inside. Second, he knew his difficult subject personally, but their differences in age and politics give him requisite objectivity. Third, he is one of the executors of Larkin's estate, so he enjoys unlimited access to all relevant material (as well as the ability to quote anything at length—an increasingly rare situation for a contemporary biographer). Finally, Motion writes well. Style and intelligence shine on every page.

Reading Motion's detailed biography, one realizes how reductive it is to label Larkin politically incorrect. If he hated immigrants, trade unions, and the Left, he also despised children, marriage, bachelors, family life, and the consolations of religion ("That vast moth-eaten musical brocade / created to pretend we never die"). He loathed the proprieties of middle-class life equally with the squalor of the poor. Public school accents made him cringe. He disliked continental Europe as much as the third world. Above all, he hated himself—his face, his body, his "filthy family," and his "bloody sodding awful life." The Elizabethans had more exact terms for this psychic state than do our contemporary pundits; they called it misanthropy and melancholy, hatred of humanity and incurable depression. By his early twenties he had already become obsessed with death. Perhaps the poet's greatest imaginative insight was to recognize these crippling liabilities in his own character and make them the basis of his art. When he made his famous quip to the press that "Deprivation is for me what daffodils were for Wordsworth," he meant it.

Larkin was born in Coventry in 1922. His domineering father was a successful accountant with progressive literary taste and fascist politics. Emotionally aloof from the family, Sydney Larkin's interest in his son was primarily intellectual; he pointed out the right books to read—Lawrence, Joyce, Hardy, and Shaw. Larkin's mother was snobbish, complaining, and ineffective. Neither parent was happy, but both were bound by duty and convention. Larkin's childhood was emotionally secure but repressed, lonely, and joyless. "We all hate home," he wrote years later in a poem, "and having to be there." He vowed early never to marry.

Larkin never left home emotionally. In late adolescence he found a new identity with his all-male friends, first in senior school and later at Oxford. They did what rebellious schoolboys always do—things their parents don't allow at home. They drank, smoked, joked obscenely, and talked about sex. They also defied the bourgeois world by writing poetry and listening to jazz. To the awkward, young Larkin, this irreverent, companionable milieu was his first taste of happiness and freedom. He never outgrew it. He never lost his schoolboy's naughty delight in profanity or conspicuous philistinism. Nor did he ever outgrow adolescence sexually.

Sex was unalloyed torture to the young Larkin. Shy and unattractive, he was impossibly clumsy with girls. He formed his lifelong opinions on sex at Oxford: "Marriage was a revolting institution." Sex wasn't worth the effort ("almost as much trouble as standing for parliament," he told his friend, novelist Kingsley Amis). Masturbation and pornography (of the tamest sort) were the lifelong mainstays of his sex life. "Sex," he consoled himself, "is too good to share with anyone else." There was not enough in Larkin's bitter bachelor's life to compensate for even the "boring, infuriating hell" of his family life. He could not live without love, and he never shook his resentful dependence on his mother. (After she died at ninety-one in 1977, Larkin soon stopped writing poetry.) His adult romances were mostly agonizing. He could not commit himself to a relationship, nor could he let go. His happiest affair was brief and adulterous. Most of the others dragged on, making everyone miserable in the process. If there was attraction and intimacy, there was also inevitably deception, anger, and regret.

If one often pities Larkin as a person, one ultimately admires him as an artist. Relentlessly introspective and self-critical, he recognized every inadequacy and failure of his humanity. Just as he constructed a charming, humorous public self to clothe his private misery, Larkin created a better version of himself in his poems. His career provides a classic illustration of the mysterious way an awful life is translated into wonderful art. "The intellect of man is forced to choose / Perfection of the life, or of the work," wrote Yeats, one of Larkin's early models. Feeling from early on that his life was doomed to unfulfillment, Larkin unambiguously chose to perfect the work. If he never stopped complaining about the emotional price of that decision, he also never flinched from it. He found a way of making the unhappiest truths darkly beautiful, of finding "Words at once true and kind, / Or not untrue and not unkind." As Motion's biography makes clear, his poems, like his letters, arose from his daily life, but in his verse he found a way of transcending his petty angers and cold self-absorption. A quietly visionary poet, he knew what life could be, even if he had rarely tasted it. His greatest poems were heartbreaking glimpses of those parts of his life that deserved to endure. "One of those old-type natural fouled-up guys," Larkin knew that in art, "What will survive of us is love."

The Two Wendy Copes

As an American reviewing a new book by Wendy Cope for a British journal, I find myself in an odd situation. In America Cope is almost unknown; in England she is too well-known. I observe this trans-Atlantic disjunction with personal embarrassment because until I undertook this review, my own assumptions about Cope's poetry combined the worst of both worlds—American ignorance and English stereotyping. Knowing a dozen or so of her poems from magazines, I had accepted the judgment of some British literary friends that Cope was a brilliant but brittle master of light verse, more parodist than poet, a Dorothy Parker *de nos jours.*

Having lived now (to my editor's increasing dismay) with Cope's three published volumes for nearly eight months, I find the conventional view of her inadequate. Cope is an altogether more original poet than either her fans or detractors make her out to be. She is, moreover, not only remarkable for her successes; she has, like Muriel Spark or Philip Larkin, the genuine writer's gift to project an imaginative world so engrossing that we even care about her failures. Cope has an extraordinarily canny sense—quite rare among poets—of what will engage a reader's attention. She has published many trivial poems and even a few downright duds, but I have yet to come across an entirely uninteresting poem. If some readers find that observation an odd compliment to pay a poet, their reaction serves as a reminder that our literati no longer expect new poetry to be interesting in the way they still demand of most prose.

Published in a substantially different version as "La Prima Donna Assoluta," review of *Serious Concerns,* by Wendy Cope, from *Poetry Review* 82.4 (winter 1992–93): 56–58.

There are two problems in evaluating Cope's new collection, *Serious Concerns*—one extraneous, the other intrinsic. The extraneous, but nonetheless unavoidable, issue is her fame. Although not a celebrity in the sense of a Madonna or Meryl Streep, Cope has achieved that modest notoriety that publishers, programmers, and journalists occasionally bestow on living poets. She has become—like Larkin or Betjeman, Sexton or Plath before her—a brand name in a literary marketplace where most poetry is dully generic. But fame inevitably requires the distortion of its subject. It must reduce the writer to a symbol or stereotype capable of existing *independently* of the poems. The mass media does not want poems; it wants, indeed craves, personalities. Marketing, likewise, abhors complexity; it demands a single, compelling point-of-difference for what it must sell, even if that product is poetry.

Reading the dust-jacket copy (and the British reviews that parrot it) from Cope's various volumes, one has no trouble in articulating Faber's "positioning" of this poet. A marketing executive could summarize it as, "For sophisticated readers who feel that contemporary poetry is boring and obscure, Wendy Cope is a refreshingly funny and accessible poet who satirizes love, sex, and literary pretension." Cope's popularity demonstrates that these are indeed compelling claims for many readers. She answers a genuine need in our insulated and inflated literary culture for the corrective perspective of satire. But Cope's ingratiating public persona obscures another, more interesting poet. And that is the other problem, the intrinsic issue in evaluating *Serious Concerns*. Which Wendy Cope should we discuss—the devastatingly accomplished satirist displaying her delectable tricks or the tentative, tender lyric poet still not sure of her identity?

Both poets appear in *Serious Concerns,* but they no longer seem on easy or equal terms. Top billing goes to Cope the satirist. She makes her dazzling entrances and exits with the calm assurance of a diva. She performs her new crowd-pleasing numbers with such *sprezzatura* that only a grump would deny her applause. Cope reminds this sober and analytical age that most poetry originates in pleasure. If her voice occasionally cracks reaching for a high note, we like her all the more for being human. But it is remarkable how few notes Cope the satirist misses. She displays formidable technique, even in her slightest performance.

If Cope now reigns as *la prima donna assoluta* of light verse, what gives her comic performances authority is their careful poetic orchestration. Light verse depends heavily on technique, but most of its practitioners are not interested in the subtleties of poetic form. They are competent versifiers who do what is necessary to realize an idea or bring off a gag. But Cope has a poet's obsession with stylistic perfection. Rereading her work, I am invariably impressed at the immense, indeed almost excessive, care with which she balances every element of texture and structure in even the most casual *jeu*. She handles versification so well in every form, from the epigram to the villanelle, from the prose poem to minimalist free verse, that one could compile a comprehensive and exemplary manual of prosody based on her work alone. Has any living poet, for example, except perhaps Donald Justice, used the villanelle so well as often? Unlike many satiric poets, Cope also demonstrates a ruthless will for compression. Her poems never go on too long. She resists the occupational hazard of light verse—padding a poem for the sake of an extra gag. But what may be Cope's most conspicuous technical accomplishment is her complete assimilation of slangy, hybrid, contemporary English into strict formal meters. This combination is one key to her accessibility: reading her, one never misses either the beat or the tone of voice.

Perhaps my praise of Cope's technical expertise is only another way of observing that parody is the surest way of absorbing the lessons of tradition. More than one critic has noticed that Cope often burlesques the poets she loves best. For the comic poet parody is often a kind of *hommage*. If Cope is an eminently accessible poet, she is also unsurpassably bookish. The wide-eyed teddy bear reading T. S. Eliot's *Notes towards the Definition of Culture*, who adorns the cover of *Serious Concerns,* deftly suggests the book's contents. Almost half the poems in Cope's volume parody, answer, echo, or overtly reflect other poems. Many of the remaining poems satirize the literary world, especially writers and publishers. Part of Cope's appeal is her candor, and among her intimate and embarrassing confessions are her unabashedly bookish habits and generally old-fashioned literary taste.

One of Cope's great strengths—her fear of boring her audience—has, however, now become a liability to her lyric poems. She no longer seems confident of her ability to spin out a story or a mood, as she did so memorably in the best work from her first collection, *Making Cocoa for Kingsley Amis*—poems like "Message," "Manifesto," or "Lonely Hearts." In many significant ways those love poems resembled her light verse. They shared the same quick, lucid, and satiric manner. Judged only by their opening lines, they would be difficult, if not sometimes impossible, to distinguish from Cope's breeziest jests. But those early lyrics allowed themselves enough room, even enough ambiguity, for their emotional subtexts to rise genie-like from between the lines and spirit them away to poetry. Those often bittersweet lyrics vividly embodied Frost's maxim that "poetry begins in delight and ends in wisdom."

Cope's "Summer Villanelle" (part of her fetching sequence "From June to December") illustrates how masterfully she employs the devices of light verse to create a poem that expands imaginatively beyond the strictures of its genre.

> You know exactly what to do—
> Your kiss, your fingers on my thigh—
> I think of little else but you.
>
> It's bliss to have a lover who,
> Touching one shoulder, makes me sigh—
> You know exactly what to do.
>
> You make me happy through and through,
> The way the sun lights up the sky—
> I think of little else but you.
>
> I hardly sleep—an hour or two;
> I can't eat much and this is why—
> You know exactly what to do.
>
> The movie in my mind is blue—
> As June runs into warm July
> I think of little else but you.
>
> But is it love? And is it true?
> Who cares? This much I can't deny:
> You know exactly what to do;
> I think of little else but you.

Stanza by stanza, "Summer Villanelle" moves in the direct, lucid, and stylish manner of light verse. The language is deliberately demotic and accessible; it never reaches for the novel phrasing or enigmatic richness that typifies much contemporary lyric poetry. The notoriously difficult sound scheme of the villanelle unfolds as if it were as natural as conversation. If, however, the verbal texture of "Summer Villanelle" resembles light verse, its narrative strategies appear provocatively poetic and its total effect both imaginatively arresting and evocatively lyric.

Neither light verse nor lyric poetry necessarily tries to portray a complete and balanced view of existence; instead, each attempts to recreate vividly and memorably the insights of a moment. If light verse customarily contracts the initiating insight into a witty summation, a lyric poem usually allows it to expand imaginatively. "Summer Villanelle" avoids the conclusive effects of wit for the quieter pleasures of exploring resonances of mood and tone. The poem trusts the authenticity of its inspiration enough to luxuriate in its subject like a languorous erotic reverie. Cope risks a few small, potentially embarrassing details (such as "your fingers on my thigh") to create an overall tone of intimacy and vulnerability. A poem like "Summer Villanelle" is infinitely harder to bring off than it appears. The language is so transparent, the subject so direct, the form so audible that any small mistake becomes amplified.

In *Serious Concerns,* however, Cope seems consistently eager for closure. "Advice to Young Women," for example, begins provocatively:

> When you're a spinster of forty,
> You're reduced to considering bids
> From husbands inclined to be naughty
> And divorcés obsessed with their kids.

This is a brilliant expository stanza, but where does it go? Cope proves unwilling to explore the poetic possibilities of the situation. Instead she immediately wraps up her theme in an expedient, generic conclusion:

So perhaps you should wed in a hurry,
But that has its drawbacks as well.
The answer? There's no need to worry—
Whatever you do, life is hell.

Clever, yes, but no more than clever. Imagine what the other Wendy Cope could have done with that opening.

It would be churlish to complain about this single poem if it did not reflect a general tendency in the new book. Her eagerness to please, her obsession to cut and condense, have conspired against her lyric sensibility. Too often she goes for the easy joke rather than truly exploring her material. One wonders whom she no longer trusts—her readers or herself? This tendency toward easy closure mars the final section of the book, which consists of serious poems on love, friends, and family, most of which are cut off before they build sufficient emotional momentum.

I make these criticisms reluctantly, worried that they will be misunderstood. I prize Cope's light verse. It displays a combination of intelligence, insight, skill, and humor too rare in contemporary poetry. It is perfect of its kind. My complaint comes from the conviction that her talent transcends that genre. Not only is there an alluring serious poet hiding behind the comic verse, but that writer had begun a particularly important enterprise—the rehabilitation of the traditional love poem.

W. H. Auden once noted that when the Romantic poets turned their attention inward to private experience, they left writers of light verse with a monopoly on the public sphere. Something similar seems to have happened with love poetry, a genre serious poets have now largely abandoned. There are still poems aplenty—affectionate, angry, and uncommitted—about marriage, divorce, betrayal, and sexual politics. But love poetry in the traditional sense of verse designed to woo, cajole, and win the beloved hardly exists today. To write love poetry one risks being labeled as "amateur" by literary "professionals." As Larkin once discovered when judging a national poetry competition, the people screening the entries discarded all the love poems before he had a chance to see them.

Cope's real originality is not in her light verse, however accomplished, but in her love poems. In *Making Cocoa for Kingsley Amis* she not only reinvented the traditional love lyric in credible, contemporary terms; she also developed an accessible but compressed lyric style that could accommodate every possible mood from silly infatuation to sexual passion, from sentimental longing to vengeful anger. In this sense the poet Cope most resembles is not Larkin, Betjeman, or Housman, but that critically unfashionable, perennially popular, and vastly underrated writer Edna St. Vincent Millay. Like Millay, Cope constructed a unifying, quasi-autobiographical persona for her poetry—a worldwise but emotionally open and intensively sexual woman. (It is surely significant that Cope had to invent a male alter ego, the grubby bohemian Jason Strugnell, to pursue themes beyond her female public persona; her instincts told her not to let her central persona go out of character, when those poems could be delegated to another fictive voice.) Like Millay, Cope also turned her personal life into an involving public myth, the ongoing odyssey of a suffering but mordant modern romantic. And, like Millay, she brought it off—in the same unexpected way, by working *against* the literary current of her time. To read Cope's best poems is not only to rediscover the power of a genre but also to remember how potent words themselves are in shaping what we love.

For that reason I will not condescend to be fair to Wendy Cope. I will not judge her new book, as a critic should, by what it actually contains—an exceptionally fine assembly of light verse. Instead I will complain unreasonably about what is not there—the lyric poems only she knows how to write. I am delighted to have one Wendy Cope, but she has made me greedy to have both.

Short Views

Ted Hughes
Kingsley Amis
Tony Connor
Dick Davis
Thom Gunn
Charles Tomlinson

Ted Hughes

For those who sat through the *cinema noir* of Ted Hughes's long poem *Gaudete* (1977), his new collection, *Moortown,* will come as a welcome relief. Once again Hughes has returned to the source of his strength as a poet, the English countryside. The only problem is that he does not stay there long enough but soon wanders off into one or another mythic landscape where the resulting poems quickly become repetitive and facile. Yet the weak sections of *Moortown* do not distract from the book's better poems because the volume is actually a collection of four distinct sections, written (as far as I can tell from Harper and Row's scanty copyright information) over a period of about ten years. Of these sections the strongest is most certainly the title sequence, which stands as one of the best things Hughes has ever written. I have always resisted the violent, sanguinary side of Hughes's imagination. In a way more typical of filmmakers like Peckinpah and DePalma than of a poet, Hughes uses sex and violence excessively in his work as a way to shock his readers into attention. The title sequence, "Moortown," is no exception to this rule. It contains enough blood, shit, piss, copulation, and afterbirth to satisfy the most scatologically minded twelve-year-old. And yet it is impossible to deny the cumulative power of the poems. Sex and violence are authentic parts of life, and these are the parts of experience that have exerted a lasting fascination for Hughes.

"Moortown" is a series of poems about a beef and sheep farm in Devon where Hughes worked with his late father-in-law, Jack Orchard. The poems chronicle a year of events on the farm against the changing backdrop of Devon. Hughes has always

Excerpt from "Poetry Chronicle," review of *Moortown*, by Ted Hughes, from the *Hudson Review* 33 (winter 1980–81): 613–14.

been drawn to writing about the nonhuman world, and so it is not surprising that the sheep, cows, and bulls dominate the poet's attention in this sequence. Hughes involves the reader so closely in a series of dramas involving animal births, deaths, diseases, and recoveries that toward the end, when he suddenly modulates into the human drama of his father-in-law's death, the effect is overwhelmingly tragic. The documentary, descriptive nature of the poem brings out a direct, unmediated pathos that shows the gentler side of Hughes's talent:

> And that is where I remember you,
> Skull-raked with thorns, sodden, tireless,
> Hauling bedded feet free, floundering away
> To check alignments, returning, hammering the staple
> Into the soaked stake oak, a careful tattoo
> Precise to the tenth of an inch,
> Under December downpour, midafternoon
> Dark as twilight, using your life up.

Unfortunately the other three sections of *Moortown* do not measure up to the achievement of the first sequence. "Prometheus on His Crag," the second section, is Hughes at his worst—strident, abstract, and portentous. This sequence is full of passages like:

> A word
>
> A bitten-out gobbet of sun
>
> Buried behind the navel, unutterable.
> The vital, immortal wound.
>
> One nuclear syllable, bleeding silence.

The third section, "Earth Numb," is a miscellany of Hughes's recent work and includes some fine individual pieces like "Bride and Groom Lie Hidden for Three Days" and "A Motorbike," but the bulk of it is mannered and strained. The last sequence, "Adam and the Sacred Nine," returns to the mythic manner of "Prometheus on His Crag" with only slightly better results. Perhaps I am deaf to the subtleties of such work, but to me it all sounds too "literary" in the worst sense of the word.

Kingsley Amis

No British poet is more unlike Ted Hughes than Kingsley Amis. Reading Hughes's *Moortown* one would never guess that more than a half dozen people live in England. Reading Amis, one cannot escape the crowds. Amis writes about England as, unfortunately, it is—a smudgy, post-industrial landscape. Likewise, while Hughes writes about Man's Fate, Amis discusses the fates of ordinary men, and he would never adopt the earnestly prophetic tone Hughes so often assumes. He does not seek the ineffable enlightenment of private vision. Instead he bases his poems on the shared perspective of common experiences. Even when he strikes an apocalyptic note, as he often does in his early work, the vision is ultimately tempered by common sense. In "The Value of Suffering" he draws an unexpected moral from the story of a nobleman who deserts his position to become a mendicant saint:

> What a shame that a regal house must founder,
> Its menials die, it favourites undergo
> Unheard-of rape, to emphasise a contrast,
> To point one thing out to one person;
> Especially since the person could have seen
> What it was all about . . .
> . . . .
> By changing places with his groom,
>   By sixty seconds' thought.

Collected Poems: 1944–1979 finally makes all of Amis's ingratiating poetry available for American readers. Looking over the volume,

Excerpt from "Poetry Chronicle," review of *Collected Poems: 1944–1979*, by Kingsley Amis, from the *Hudson Review* 33 (winter 1980–81): 614–16.

it is interesting to trace the author's development over those thirty-five years and compare him to his close friend and contemporary Philip Larkin. In the mid-fifties Amis and Larkin must have seemed very much alike as writers. Both of them were novelists who had also written a small, carefully crafted body of poetry. Yet by the mid-sixties it was clear that Amis had chosen the role of a minor poet while Larkin had become one of the best poets writing in English. It was not that Amis's work had declined in quality. For Amis proved Auden's dictum that minor poetry is as well written as major poetry. Nor was it solely that Amis poured his genius into his novels and his talent into his verse. Instead, his development seems primarily temperamental. Amis chose the role of anti-romantic in his poetry, and he has lived with that decision and its consequences. Larkin may debunk romanticism in his poetry, but there is a visionary note underlying his best work. In contrast Amis never gives in to what used to be called "the oceanic feeling." Amis never loses a sense of distance from his subject, even when it is himself. In "A Dream of Fair Women," one of his finest poems, he explores his own sexual fantasies in a formal set piece about an imaginary bordello that makes its revelations indirectly through wit and diction rather than bald confession:

> Militant all, they fight to take my hat,
> No more as yet; the other men retire
>   Insulted, gestured at;
> Each girl presses on me her share of what
> Makes up the barn-door target of desire:
>   And I am a crack shot.
>
> Speech fails them, amorous, but each one's look,
> Endorsed in other ways, begs me to sign
>   Her body's autograph book;
> "Me first, Kingsley; I'm cleverest" each declares,
> But no gourmet races downstairs to dine,
>   Nor will I race upstairs.

Amis may limit himself by dwelling within the "temperate zone" of experience, but within these latitudes he writes with memorable precision and zest. He demonstrates a lesson it is too easy to forget—that to write well about ordinary events takes extra-ordinary skill. And so in its peculiar way, Amis's *Collected Poems* is a necessary book, especially for those American readers who do not share his anti-romantic assumption that intelligence, wit, form, and verbal ingenuity are the essentials of poetry. Readers who find Rimbaud, Whitman, Ginsberg, and Snyder especially sympathetic can be assured that in this sense at least Amis's work will prove a mind-expanding experience.

Tony Connor

How good it is to have Tony Connor's *New and Selected Poems.*
Connor's books have never been easy to get in the United
States, and he has inexplicably been omitted from most an-
thologies, so this new volume will provide most Americans their
first chance to read his work at length. I suspect that they will
find much to enjoy here. Connor is an unusual poet from an un-
likely background, and his work is both original and entertain-
ing. Born in a working-class family in Lancashire in 1930, Con-
nor left school at fourteen and embarked on a series of jobs to
help support his mother and sister (his "swindler, con-man, and
embezzler" father having run away to avoid arrest when the
poet was five). Connor worked as paperboy, textile designer,
cake decorator, and army tank driver before gradually estab-
lishing himself first as poet, then as television writer, and later
(in America) as professor of poetry *sans* degree.

I mention the facts of Connor's life because he himself makes
so much of them. Most of his work is openly autobiographical.
His early poems depict working-class life in Lancashire in the
lean years after the Second World War, with much attention
being directed at his own troubled family, especially the father
he scarcely knew. When most poets open up about their child-
hood sorrows, the reader is tempted to close the book, for he or
she knows a torrent of trivial memories and petty injustices
vaguely shaped to resemble poems is about to pour forth. Not so
with Connor. His family poems, like "My Father's Walking-Stick,"
are hard, concise, and unsentimental. While one feels they pre-
sent the events of Connor's childhood very candidly, they never

---

Excerpt from "Poetry Chronicle," review of *New and Selected Poems,* by
Tony Connor, from the *Hudson Review* 35 (winter 1982–83): 648–50.

degenerate into mere confession, for the poet does not share the fashionable assumption that experience itself is a substitute for imagination. Too often autobiographical poets try to stun their readers into submission, stridently asserting, "This is true! This really happened!" As if the shock of reality could compensate for the crudity of the retelling. Connor does not simply report events. He vividly recreates them, shaping each scene with the skill and care of a novelist.

Connor's early work is also full of poems which use his class and regional background to create memorable pictures of his own time and place. Perhaps his best poem is "Elegy for Alfred Hubbard," a portrait of a half-incompetent old Lancashire plumber. (Curiously, although this poem is not well-known in this country, it has been skillfully plagiarized by at least two American poets.) Another remarkable Lancashire poem is "Mrs. Root," which presents a neighborhood busybody obsessed with marriages and funerals. But Connor's interests are not limited by his regional background. Poems like "An Anonymous Painting" and "A Journal of Bad Times" reflect a broad cultural perspective. The only real complaint with Connor's *New and Selected Poems* is that the book is too short, and the selection overemphasizes his autobiographical poetry at the expense of his other work. Where, for example, is "Child's Bouncing Song," an ingenious piece of nonsense verse based on playground chants? Did either the poet or his editor deem this little gem not serious enough for inclusion? Where, too, is his "Fashionable Poet Reading," a devastating portrait of a pompous literary mediocrity? The inclusion of more poems like these would show the full range of Connor's accomplishment. Connor is not a technically adventurous poet, but when his poems require it he can manage widely different styles with equal ease. On one page he can describe a "Lancashire Winter" in witty, all-knowing rhymed stanzas:

> The town remembers no such plenty,
> under the wind from off the moor.
> The labour exchange is nearly empty;
> stiletto heels on the Palais floor
> move between points of patent leather.
> Sheepskin coats keep out the weather.

Commerce and Further Education
won't be frozen. Dully free
in snack bars and classrooms sits the patient
centrally heated peasantry . . .

Only a few pages before he had used long, free verse lines (with a strong accentual base) and disjointed syntax to create a mysterious sense of social dislocation in "A Journal of Bad Times":

In Autumn, begin.
                          Uprooting geraniums,
shaking them gently for storage in darkness,
had heard guns crackle in far streets.
In the deepening sky, one evening,
a plane wrote "Freedom"—a vaporous trail
gone before sunset.
                          Beyond the city, mountains—
most often hidden. On clear days certain fields,
a pike, glinting glass. Many went that way,
wheels rumbling towards rock.
                          None saw a good end.

In recent years Connor's work has not changed substantially in either subject or style. The thirty new poems in his volume still explore themes familiar from his earlier books, though many of them now have an American backdrop. "Reduced to a man of sense," he has developed no vatic pretensions in middle age, and his work remains clear-headed, intelligent, and immensely readable. Two recent poems deserve special note: "Reminiscences Remembered," a witty portrait of an irreverent old bard making the university circuit (which must be at least partially based on Basil Bunting), and the volume's final poem, "'And leave the voice of commerce blaring through an empty house,'" which leaves a tantalizing suggestion of what Connor may be up to in the future.

Why bother to write at all,
with no mouthing oracle

at the ear of my study,
where I sit at the ready?

Reduced to a man of sense,
why need I nurture silence?

More useful to emulate
the folks next door, Fran and Dwight,

whose loud FM receiver
misses no bargain offer,

who rush to far discount stores
in their end-of-year-sale cars,

and leave the voice of commerce
blaring through an empty house.

Dick Davis

Reading Dick Davis's new book, *Seeing the World,* confirms my impression that he is one of the two or three best young poets now writing in England. With only two thin books to his credit, Davis is already a fully realized poet. There is no mistaking one of his poems. More than any other English poet of his generation, Davis has created a distinctly personal voice, an accomplishment all the more impressive because he has chosen to work in a controlled, classical style. He never cultivates idiosyncrasies, and yet one can always recognize a Davis poem by the intensity of his imagination and the deceptive simplicity of his words. In an age when American and British English are drifting further apart, Davis is also remarkable in how fully his poems are audible to an American ear. I can hear (or at least have the illusion I can hear) everything that is going on in a Davis poem, whereas I simply cannot hear the subtleties in the poems of so many of his countrymen—even highly praised poets I have read many times, such as W. S. Graham and C. H. Sisson.

Davis's poems are usually very short and straightforward. They are highly condensed, but the sensuous surface is so smoothly polished that one never notices how much is going on until the poem is reread carefully. The platitude one hears bandied around so often in poetry textbooks—that every word must contribute to the total effect—is literally true in a Davis poem, and yet the effect never seems labored or contrived. Take for example his seemingly relaxed poem "Government in Exile." Could one remove half a line without substantially changing the movement and meaning of the poem?

Excerpt from "Poetry Chronicle," review of *Seeing the World,* by Dick Davis, from the *Hudson Review* 32 (winter 1980–81): 616–17.

Silence, and on the wall the photographs—
Farms, mountains, faces; the sad specifics
Corrode the heart, sharpen the will. Despair
Is shrugged away and stares one in the face.

Loyalty is poured out—a libation
To childhood villages, to stones, to trees.

With this gift for brevity and grace under pressure it is not surprising that Davis has turned his attention to the epigram. What is surprising, however, is that he has turned away from the conventional image of the epigram as satiric form *à la* X. J. Kennedy or J. V. Cunningham (to name the two great American masters of the form) and has returned to the ancient notion of short, serious lyrics compressed into a few lines. He has abandoned the tradition of Martial for the example of the *Greek Anthology*. The results are often compelling short poems quite unlike anything else in contemporary English literature.

See where the landscape glows and flares
Lit by the beacons of desire—

As faces grouped about a fire
Give back the light that is not theirs.

("False Light")

This obsession to condense experience and language into tight, controlled forms is matched by Davis's need to establish a moral dimension in his poetry. Morality for him seems to be an organizing principle as important as meter or diction. In some ways all three principles may even be different sides of the same vision of poetry. Implicitly or explicitly in almost every piece, poetry becomes a moral judgment of experience. Some readers will clearly resist a sensibility so certain of its mission, but a mind that can recreate and evaluate a scene in a few memorable lines deserves attention in this garrulous age.

Thom Gunn

Poetry must be magnificently achieved, or it is negligible. Few writers manage to sustain the special verbal and emotional intensity that poetry requires across their whole career. Even great poets, like William Wordsworth or Samuel Taylor Coleridge, often falter after a decade or two of extraordinary writing. But Thom Gunn has kept writing in top form for five decades. Although he began with such youthful ferocity that he seemed destined to burn out early, his later work has only grown in scope and power. No other poet has so vividly captured so much of Bay Area experience—from San Francisco street life to the surrounding natural world.

It may seem paradoxical, but San Francisco's best living poet is a British citizen. The contradictions that make up Thom Gunn, however, don't stop with his passport. Gunn's particular genius has been to embody the human and artistic contradictions of his age. Reading his extravagantly diverse *Collected Poems* (1994), one finds poems on LSD, video games, and street hustlers next to lyrics on Catholic saints, Keats, and Caravaggio—all of them not only perfectly achieved but recognizably drawn from the same imagination. Gunn is the crown prince of incongruity, a Romantic entranced by classical control, an experimentalist who never renounced rhyme and meter, an antiauthoritarian populist by mandarin standards.

When Gunn first came to the Bay Area in 1954, he was only twenty-five but had already published a celebrated book of poems. Having won a writing fellowship at Stanford, the young gay poet with "a promiscuous love of experience" studied with the famously rigorous Yvor Winters, a brilliant but cantankerous

Published as "Top Gunn," from *San Francisco*, December 1999, 63.

poet-critic. What could have been a destructive collision between two strong-willed and temperamentally different minds became instead a warm and productive friendship between mentor and student. Gunn's already incisive style sharpened under Winters's formalist tutelage, but his tone and subject kept their rebellious edge. His second book, for instance, began with a poem in rhymed iambic pentameter stanzas about a motorcycle gang on the move.

Gunn's greatest moment as a poet came at his most difficult time—the AIDS epidemic that devastated San Francisco. In one month alone he lost four close friends. Out of this personal and public crisis grew *The Man with the Night Sweats* (1992), which will probably stand as the central poetic testament of those plague years. While most AIDS poetry relies on naked grief and raw emotion, Gunn's tough lyric meditations are simultaneously realistic and transcendent, as in his title poem, which begins:

> I wake up cold, I who
> Prospered through dreams of heat
> Wake to their residue,
> Sweat, and a clinging sheet.

Now seventy, Gunn retired last spring from U.C. Berkeley, where he taught intermittently over forty years. (He willingly gave up tenure in 1966 to be free to teach under his own terms.) Looking less like a retired professor than an emeritus rock star, Gunn still lives, as he has for decades, in the Cole Valley district. Casual, worldly, and observant, Gunn is not defiantly youthful but effortlessly ageless—not unlike the city that has been his muse.

Charles Tomlinson

Charles Tomlinson has probably learned more from America than any living British poet. As an undergraduate, he read Moore, Stevens, and Pound—hardly fashionable authors at Cambridge in the late forties—and became fascinated with their novel sense of poetic structure and style. Williams's influence came a little later, and Tomlinson soon adapted the three-part line and many of Williams's other rhythmic innovations into his own work. For most English poets American free verse is more dangerous than whiskey. But Tomlinson managed to assimilate his modern masters without becoming imitative just as he has been able to write persuasively about so many foreign landscapes without seeming touristic. While many of his English contemporaries retreated to local themes and native traditions, he steadfastly looked abroad, first to America and then to Europe and Japan. He is a postmodernist par excellence—deeply conscious of the international Modern tradition but still deeply himself.

America's influence on Tomlinson has not only been literary. He has lived and traveled extensively in this country, and his books are full of poems which scrupulously recreate places in America most natives don't know. *The Flood* alone contains poems about out-of-the-way cities like Jemez, Quarai, Cochiti, Cronkhite Beach, and Poolville, as well as a few well-known ones like San Francisco and Albuquerque. When most Englishmen write about America, it ceases to be a real place and becomes a myth. Tomlinson never misses the reality. His poems vividly cap-

Excerpt from "Poetry Chronicle," review of *The Flood*, by Charles Tomlinson, and *Airborn / Hijos del Aire*, by Octavio Paz and Charles Tomlinson, from the *Hudson Review* 34 (winter 1981–82): 581–84.

ture the presence of a place. American poets have been trying to write poems like "Mr. Brodsky" or "Arroyo Hondo" for years. Tomlinson seems to do it effortlessly.

The Flood marks no new breakthrough for Tomlinson. Rather it is a deepening of themes developed in his earlier books. Most of the poems describe the places one associates with the author—Italy, New Mexico, and Gloucestershire, where he now lives. Yet there is no sense of repetition. Though the places may by now be familiar, the inspiration behind the new poems is fresh and genuine. Tomlinson has often written about the coast of Italy, but "San Fruttuoso: the divers" is still a revelation. The author's eye for precise detail catches just those elements which made one day in that city unique.

Tomlinson is an artist as well as a poet, and his critics usually label him as a visual poet, one who uses close observation of the natural world as the basis of what one might literally call his artistic vision. Certainly Tomlinson has a sharp eye for images, but to consider him primarily a painter with words misses the most distinctive thing about his work—its sound. One can always recognize one of his poems (a hard claim to make for most English poets), whatever its subject, whether it is in free or formal verse. Even the unusual passage in couplets below has so many of the sounds one associates with him—the rapid pace, the continual spilling over of sentences from line to line, the nonchalant introduction of a foreign expression, the deft variation between groups of monosyllabic and polysyllabic words, the restless syntax that moves with his equally restless imagination:

> Are you the swift that dips here, or the course
> 　　Of sheer, unimpeded water, the counterforce
> Of rock and stone? But images lie—
> 　　Not the Ding-an-sich, but the light to see it by:
> And no river could convey the artifice
> 　　And no landscape either, the pulse of this:
> A closer thing, it is as if thought might sing
> 　　To the bloodbeat, set it racing.
>
> 　　　　　　　　　　　　　　　　("Programme Note")

The last four poems in the book describe the Severn River, which flows near Tomlinson's home in Gloucestershire, and a relentless winter storm that climaxed in a flood which overran his cottage. The title poem feverishly recounts the last nights before the home was flooded. Even as he frantically worked to divert the water, Tomlinson could not help but be fascinated by the power of the river, and toward the end there is a wonderful moment when the poet comes downstairs the morning afterward to view his ruined home:

> Full morning
> Floated and raced with water through the house,
>   Dancing in whorls on every ceiling
> As I advanced. Sheer foolishness
>   It seemed to pause and praise the shimmer
> And yet I did and called you down
>   To share this vertigo of sunbeams everywhere,
> As if no surface were safe from swaying
>   And the very stone were as malleable as clay.

I hope that Tomlinson will share more such "foolishness" with us in the future.

Along with *The Flood,* Tomlinson has also published an unusual bilingual book written in collaboration with the Mexican poet Octavio Paz. *Airborn / Hijos del Aire* consists of two short sequences of unrhymed sonnets, each written around a central theme—"House" and "Day." The poets collaborated by writing alternate stanzas of each poem—Tomlinson in English, Paz in Spanish—which the other would then translate (thereby making the collaboration even more complex). Each sequence then ends with a poem written entirely by one poet (which, of course, is then immediately translated by the other). It all sounds like a lost novella by Nabokov, but the result is a remarkable little book.

Tomlinson and Paz are both fascinated with collaborative poetry, especially the linked verse of Japanese literature. (Their previous effort, *Renga,* in 1971, involved four poets working in four languages.) After reading *Renga,* I thought that such collaborations were doomed to be interesting curiosities. Yet *Airborn* comes so close to success that I now believe it may be possible to bring off these Japanese forms in a contemporary Western context. The best poem in the book is the one written entirely by Paz, but many of the others do work well in a curious way. The act of reading this poetry is very different from reading traditional texts. Here one is always conscious of the transitions from one poet to the next. Will Paz be able to follow the challenge of Tomlinson's stanza? Will Tomlinson be able to develop the images of Paz's opening lines? One cannot read these poems without continually judging whether one poet has built successfully on what came before. It is exciting, exhausting reading that challenges one's notion of what a poem (and a translation) really is.

For example, Paz begins one poem in the "House" section with a complex stanza that simultaneously recalls his own childhood home, which no longer exists except in memory, and also suggests that the poems he is now writing have become a kind of shared imaginary home for the two poets:

> *House that memory makes out of itself*
> *between the spaces of blank time—more thought*
> *than lived and yet more said than thought,*
> *house that lasts as long as its own sound takes:*

In Tomlinson's continuation one can't help noticing how the imagery becomes more concrete, the idea of the house less Platonic and more Proustian:

> house, you began in milk, in warmth, in eating:
> words must re-tongue your first solidities
> and thought keep fresh your fragrance of bread baking
> or drown in the stagnation of its memories:

One could ask whether this is a continuation of Paz's opening or an entirely new poem. Something in between, the authors would probably reply, and, whatever that something is, it's worth looking into.

The Novelist as Poet

Anthony Burgess was a novelist of indisputable genius who never published an indisputably great novel. Some writers—like Ralph Ellison or Giuseppe di Lampedusa—labor endlessly to focus their full imagination into a single masterpiece. Burgess lavishly spread his gifts across thirty-three novels of startling diversity. He left no *magnum opus* but scored nearly a dozen brilliant near-misses. His best novels show such scope, intelligence, and extravagant originality that many readers share Gore Vidal's assessment that Burgess was "easily the most interesting English writer in the last half century."

Burgess's last novel, *Byrne,* is not, alas, the masterpiece that long eluded him. This new volume, however, is so fresh, funny, and inventive that it ranks among his finest creations. Completed shortly before his death in 1993, *Byrne* demonstrates that not only was Burgess's artistry undiminished at the end but it was still growing. Many of his books have an experimental shape, but none is more boldly designed than *Byrne,* which unfolds in an entirely new form for Burgess—the verse novel.

Most novelists have a youthful fling with poetry before settling down sensibly with prose, but Burgess never lost his early passion. He published an epic poem and undertook half a dozen major verse translations ranging from *Oedipus the King* to *Cyrano de Bergerac.* He also repeatedly placed poets—Shakespeare, Marlowe, Keats—as the central figures in his novels. Even his most popular comic character, the constipated F. X. Enderby, was a

Published as "Deathbed Confession," review of *Byrne,* by Anthony Burgess, from the *New York Times Book Review,* November 30, 1997, 9–10. The comments on Burgess's Belli translations are an excerpt from "Poetry Chronicle," from the *Hudson Review* 34 (winter 1981–82): 593–94.

poet. (Burgess filled his four Enderby novels with copious verses purportedly written by his maladroit protagonist.)

In principle one had to admire Burgess's ambitious rejection of literary specialization. Why shouldn't a novelist also work in poetry or verse drama? In practice, however, the reader faced a serious problem. Burgess's poetry was vastly inferior to his prose. Ostentatiously inventive and original, his prose in novels like *A Clockwork Orange* or *Nothing Like the Sun* was not only delightful but dazzlingly effective. In contrast, his verse seemed, like poor Mr. Enderby, cramped and costive.

Mindful of these failings, I picked up *Byrne* with trepidation. What I found was genuinely astonishing—a complex dark comedy in fluently rhymed verse. Frequently hilarious and always engaging, this final book simultaneously satisfies the differing demands of prose fiction and narrative verse. Composed mostly in the same ottava rima stanza that Lord Byron used for *Don Juan, Byrne* shows Burgess for once fully in command of his poetic medium. One might expect an author to experience new spiritual insight on his deathbed, but surely such a technical breakthrough is highly unusual.

Despite its singular form, *Byrne* is an entirely characteristic Burgess novel. It examines his central themes—sex, religion, art, and mortality—though with an urgency seldom found in earlier books. The protagonist is once again an imaginary artist, in this case Michael Byrne, a minor modern composer with greater talent in bed than in the concert hall. The novel's opening section recounts Byrne's public and private careers. "Failed artist but successful bigamist," he moves opportunistically from country to country and from bed to bed, leaving a small tribe of children across the globe. Eventually Byrne vanishes, presumably dying of old age in Africa.

The second section shifts abruptly to the present and focuses on several of Byrne's children, now in late middle age. To their astonishment, they discover that their notorious father is still alive. He has publicly invited "the fruits of his insemination / legitimate or not" to a Christmas Eve gathering at Claridges, where he will read his final will and testament. The rest of *Byrne* tells of the complicated and violent paths his children take to this nightmarish reunion.

Perhaps the novel's most striking episode is Byrne's sojourn in Nazi Germany. Leaving London with an aging Teutonic diva, Byrne enters the upper echelons of Berlin Kultur. He recognizes Nazi racial theories as rubbish, but the amoral adventurer also notes the professional opportunities afforded an Aryan composer in Germany's newly *Judenfrei* musical world. Soon Byrne writes an operatic showpiece for his soprano lover set to a libretto by Joseph Goebbels. Burgess brilliantly counterpoints the composer's personal indifference to the nightmarish milieu of the age. As Byrne labors on his ambitious opera, he even finds distractions in the increasingly brutal society around him:

> A heavy task, but there was light relief
> In the Germanic ambience, boisterous, brash,
> Torchlit parades and pogroms, guttural grief
> In emigration queues, the smash and crash
> Of pawnshop windows by insentient beef
> In uniform, the gush of beer, the splash
> Of schnapps, the joy of being drunk and Aryan,
> Though Hitler was a teetotalitarian.

Alternately hilarious and bitter, the opening section stands as one of the finest things Burgess ever wrote. A self-consciously literary artist, Burgess customarily built his novels in layers. A comic plot might be set upon a theological allegory and then refracted again through an unreliable narrator. *Byrne* proceeds in a similar manner. The first section is simultaneously a mock biography of a failed Modernist and a scathing critique of art's relations and responsibilities to society—all told, we eventually discover, by a journalist who may himself be one of Byrne's deserted illegitimate children.

If the later sections do not sustain the comic brilliance of the opening, they still read very well. Only the ending disappoints. Patterning his climax after the harrowing conclusion of Conrad's *The Heart of Darkness*, Burgess miscalculates. Significantly, the problem is prosodic as well as narrative. The author allows the superannuated and demented Byrne to read his last will in five gnomic sonnets. The poem's narrative momentum founders at just the moment it needs to hold swift and steady.

The poetic style of *Byrne* might reasonably be termed Byronic if it didn't also sound exactly like Burgess. Not the least of the book's accomplishments is a richly textured verse style that fully accommodates the quirky particulars of the novelist's voice. Shedding the lofty models who had so often inhibited his early poetry—especially Gerard Manley Hopkins and T. S. Eliot—Burgess finally permitted himself to write verse that didn't strive to be poetic. Instead, *Byrne* marries the novelistic virtues of energetic narrative and social observation with "old-fashioned rhyme." The result is a tangy style that combines the author's earthy sensibility with the compression and evocative musicality of formal verse. When Byrne, currently a film composer, weds a fellow employee at the Korda brothers' London studios, Burgess sums up the marriage in a single well-turned stanza:

> He married Brenda Brown, who worked in make-up
> —A cosmetician: God was not much more
> (*Kosmetikos* from *kosmos*)—keen to take up
> Domestic calm he once had thought a bore.
> She was a decent girl who did not rake up
> Harsh details of the life he'd lived before.
> Happy in Morden, mortgaged, half-detached,
> He fertilised her eggs. They duly hatched.

If *Byrne* is a novel built in layers, no one familiar with Burgess's life and career can fail to recognize that one layer is autobiographical. The two main characters—Byrne and his son Tim—are both unflattering versions of the author. Tim, a faithless priest, hopes to make a secular living by writing religious documentaries for American Protestants. (In his final years Burgess wrote Biblical miniseries for American networks.) Midway through the novel Tim provides a more disturbing parallel. He begins coughing blood, only to discover—as Burgess did—that he is dying of lung cancer. As a medieval monk might place a skull on his writing desk as a *memento mori,* Burgess put his own dying body into his final book.

Equally chilling are the parallels with Byrne himself. This Anglo-Irish, lapsed-Catholic artist bears many obvious resemblances to his Anglo-Irish, lapsed-Catholic creator. In interviews

Burgess, an internationally successful novelist, critic, screen-writer, and translator, habitually described himself as "a failed composer." (Until writing his first novel at thirty-eight, he had concentrated on music and continued to compose throughout his life.) *Byrne* is an extended meditation on an artist whose work has come to nothing. Byrne's music will make no claim on posterity. Even his profligate sexuality proved futile. All of his scattered sons and daughters are childless. As the narrator admits, the future will bring only oblivion to his depraved protagonist:

> The fascination of the reprehensible
> Is my true driving force—was, I should say.
> There's no defending of the indefensible,
> No armature to strengthen feet of clay.
> Wretches like Byrne are far from indispensable,
> A single puff will blow their dust away.
> Paronomasia is a needless joke:
> He needs no fire to turn him into smoke.

"Paronomasia" is a typical Burgessian touch. (The word is the rhetorical term for a pun.) Even contemplating the possibility of his own physical and artistic extinction, the author revels in the power of language. Perhaps it will be just that deep impulse of delight in the face of human finitude that will keep posterity reading Burgess.

❧

Anyone who has crossed the Tiber from central Rome into Trastevere has probably seen a statue that seems to stand guard at the entrance of the district. It is of a seated man in a top hat and cloak and bears the enviable inscription:

> To Their Poet
> G. G. Belli
> The People of Rome

Giuseppe Gioachino Belli (1791–1863) is a unique figure in Italian literature. Joyce and Sainte-Beuve praised him. Lawrence and Gogol wanted to translate him. Anthony Burgess made him the protagonist of his novel *ABBA ABBA*. Belli was the greatest Roman satirist since Juvenal. His vast work captured every aspect of Roman life from the papacy to the police, from the booksellers to the bordellos. He is the definitive author of Rome, a comic genius, like Joyce with Dublin, whose work embraced a great modern city and its people. And yet Belli, a poet of European stature, remains little read, even in Italy. The reason for his obscurity is obvious—his language. His twenty-two hundred sonnets are not written in standard literary Italian but in Romanesco, the Roman dialect. By writing in Romanesco, Belli effectively limited his audience to the citizens of one city.

The best versions of Belli in English are the seventy-one sonnets that Burgess attached as an appendix to *ABBA ABBA*. They are sometimes wild, but they capture Belli's brilliant satiric tone. Compare the opening stanza of Belli's famous "Er Giorno der Giudizzio," a half-irreverent, half-serious vision of the Judgment Day, in two translations. First is Miller Williams's version, which ambitiously recreates the form of the original:

> Each of four huge angels wraps his mouth
> Around a trumpet and then he begins to blow,
> One to the north, the east, the west, the south;
> A voice says, "Step right up." First thing you know . . .

Now here is Burgess's version (yes, it is a translation of the same poem):

> At the round earth's imagined corners let
> Angels regale us with a brass quartet,
> Capping that concord with a fourfold shout:
> "Out everybody, everybody out!"

Burgess's version has wit and verve. He has translated Belli into poetry and caught the brusque apocalyptic humor of the original. Strangely enough, though Burgess changes the rhyme scheme and quotes John Donne, his version is not much further from the Italian than Miller Williams's more literal translation, which considerably changes one line as well as misses the witty closure of the original stanza. Why translate Belli into English sonnets if one doesn't use the form to advantage? Belli enthusiasts will want to acquire Burgess's versions—or pray that Giacomo Joyce will quickly dictate his version to us from the Great Beyond via James Merrill's ouija board.

Donald Davie's Imaginary Museum

The Poet in the Imaginary Museum is a long-overdue collection of essays and reviews by the British poet and critic Donald Davie. The selections in the volume span most of Davie's very active career, beginning with a review written in England in 1950 and ending with an essay written in California in 1977. Inexplicably the volume is subtitled *Essays of Two Decades* though it explicitly covers nearly thirty years of work. Yet one is inclined to excuse the faultiest arithmetic when the same mind produces such excellent writing. For *The Poet in the Imaginary Museum* is an important book containing some of the most penetrating essays on modern poetry written in the thirty years it covers. It calls to mind as fine a book as Randall Jarrell's *Poetry and the Age* for comparison (a book coincidentally published in 1953, just as Davie's career as a critic was beginning); as well as any book since Jarrell's collection, *The Poet in the Imaginary Museum* defines the situation, climate, and limits of contemporary poetry.

Davie would probably not cherish the comparison to Jarrell (a poet whom he does not admire), but the similarities are real and important ones. Both Jarrell and Davie insist on seeing the poet as a member of society. Though both of them excel in close readings, they place the writer cautiously against his time and place before turning to the poems themselves for appraisal. Likewise both of them search the lives and backgrounds of authors for crucial clues to their writing. If Jarrell dwells more on time and Davie more on place, it is only a matter of emphasis.

Published as "A Personal Tour of Donald Davie's Imaginary Museum," review of *The Poet in the Imaginary Museum: Essays of Two Decades,* by Donald Davie, edited and introduced by Barry Alpert, from the *Southern Review* 15 (summer 1979): 724–29.

Most important, both of them refuse to write criticism only for other critics. They long for a mixed audience of poets, academics, students, and general readers, and, if this audience still exists for poetry, it is largely due to efforts like theirs. Jarrell once asked for a type of criticism which would not only be intelligent and useful but also "sound as if it has been written by a reader for readers, by a human being for human beings." He would have approved of Davie. For Davie is a specialist who can speak to the general reader without condescension. And none of Davie's volumes demonstrates this ability better than *The Poet in the Imaginary Museum*. Though some of its contents were written in the most popular and ephemeral genres of literary criticism (radio lectures and book reviews), and other parts written for the most specialized scholarly publications (*Paideuma, Twentieth Century Literature, Poetics*), virtually all of the essays and articles remain engaging and approachable for all types of readers. That alone is an achievement worth applauding.

Davie and his editor, Barry Alpert, made two interesting decisions in assembling *The Poet in the Imaginary Museum*. First, they restricted themselves to selections from only one part of Davie's considerable critical writings, those on twentieth-century poetry and poetics. Of the forty-six pieces in the volume, only one, a review of Beckett, is not concerned with modern poetry or poetics. Second, Davie apparently designed the book to present his reviews and essays as an ongoing record of the contemporary poetic scene, reprinting everything exactly as it first appeared (though in some cases he has affixed a postscript, usually to clarify or retract his original opinion). Both editorial decisions pay off. The focus on modern poetry not only reveals the major direction of Davie's career; it also makes this volume not so much a miscellany as a unified survey of twentieth-century poetry in English. Meanwhile, the decision to reprint the essays without revisions and to attach postscripts turns what might have been a very austere collection into a personable journal recounting an important poet's attempt to clarify his position in relation to the immediate past and his contemporaries.

To say that the essays in *The Poet in the Imaginary Museum* all deal with modern poetry and poetics almost seems too narrow a definition, for Davie insists on discussing poetry in the broadest possible context. Repeatedly throughout the book, he compares poetry to the other modern arts and contrasts the position of the modern poet to that of painters, composers, and sculptors. Davie's striking conclusion is that the modern poet is the odd man out. While the other arts have grown more wide-reaching and international through the developments of modern technology—color photography, cinematography, phonographic recording, and even jet air travel—poetry has largely stayed at home, grounded by its native language and national cultural associations. In the volume's title essay Professor Davie describes the poet's dilemma in the following terms:

> So it comes about that the poet's situation is peculiarly difficult; in so far as poetry shares in "a modern movement" common to all the arts (and it seems plain that to some extent it does so share, feeling the impact, no less than the other arts, of modern anthropology, for instance), the poet shares with the other artists a new attitude towards the cultural and artistic past of the race, a new freedom in picking and choosing among the styles of the past. Yet in so far as the medium of poetry is not international as the other media are, the poet finds himself less free of the riches of the past than the painter is, if only because most of the poems of the past are in languages he does not understand. Thus the poet stands awkwardly with one foot inside the imaginary museum, and one foot out of it.

Such a passage is typical of Davie's interest. He combines the roles of cultural commentator and literary critic in his prose. He describes his modern poet both as an individual and as a citizen of a certain nation, the child of his own time and place. While his problem is the collective dilemma of his culture, his solution must be individual. This passage can also be seen as autobiographical. The poet Davie describes is himself. The problem is the situation he faced as a young academic poet writing in England in the fifties. His escape from the confines of nationalism included his emigration to America. He internationalized himself within the limits his native English language would allow.

One of Davie's enduring concerns has been the relationship between the poet and his readers, a set of assumptions by the artist that Davie often expands into the relationship between a writer and his society. Recent critics have made elaborate claims that the American poetic imagination is essentially autistic. Against this background, it is helpful to find Davie's more straightforward distinction between much modern British and American poetry, explained in terms of the poet's rhetoric, not metaphysics:

> For the English poet the writing of poems is a public and so-cial activity, as for his American peer it isn't. . . . For the sad fact is that English readers of contemporary poetry—few as they are, and perhaps just *because* they are so few—have got used to being cajoled and coaxed, at all events sedulously *attended to,* by their poets.

While Davie laments the congeniality of his contemporaries, an American reader might long for poets who can be approached on such comfortable terms. One suspects that Davie might be sympathetic with such an American, for, after all, perhaps his point is that the best poetry is somewhere in the middle—poetry which is intended as public speech but does not become loose and flabby in response to a lazy audience. Davie has certainly sought this blend in his poetry. In moving to America he consciously tried to create a poetic style which kept the distinctively British sense of an audience and a tradition while acquiring the scope, the concentration, and the public-be-damned integrity of the American poetry he most admires.

This poetic search also benefited Davie's prose. In his books, essays, and reviews he also searched for what was alive and useful in both the American and the British traditions. His critical work was full of an energy and personality hardly typical of most academic writing of the fifties and sixties, because for Davie criticism had become an act of self-discovery, and the trans-Atlantic exchange was the crucial unknown element. For personal reasons he had to create an audience which could understand both sides. It is hardly surprising then that more than any other contemporary critic Davie has been the one who helped put British and American poetry back on speaking terms. Davie has not only introduced dozens of American poets to an initially suspicious and insular British public; he has also demanded the attention of chauvinistic American readers to the best contemporary English writing. In making these exchanges he has revealed his taste as remarkably independent and catholic. What other British critic could have made such a convincing case for the necessity of importing talents as diverse as Yvor Winters, George Oppen, Edward Dorn, Samuel Menashe, and Edgar Bowers—all poets not terribly well-known even in America? Likewise who else could have made such a suavely compelling plea for Americans to read Betjeman, Larkin, Tomlinson, Bunting, and Sisson? *The Poet in the Imaginary Museum* documents Davie's continuous efforts to make the two nations hear each other talking. And if now American and British poets are communicating on equal terms for perhaps the first time in history, it is as much due to Davie as to any other poet or critic living. Occasionally he even gets some of the credit.

This credit has been hard-won. At the beginning of his career Davie found himself in an ironic position. Pushed into the public limelight as a member of The Movement, a group of British poets who insisted on the continuing vitality of native traditions and on the incompatibility of modern experimentalism with English genius, the personally conservative Davie gradually emerged as an apologist both for foreign poetry and for experimental writing. His sense of himself as an Englishman was always strong enough not be threatened by foreign cultures. He translated Mickiewicz, Pasternak, Bassani, and Mandelstam in ways that made them accessible to English readers. He carefully demonstrated the relevance of the modern masters like Pound and Valéry to his contemporaries. While proving the centrality of Hardy and Graves to the modern English tradition, he also secured Olson, Bunting, and Winters a place on the required reading list. The criticism which accomplished this sleight of hand is certainly a model of agility. Davie simultaneously convinced his audience that he was the one member of this generation most capable of defining the living traditions in English literature while vigorously preaching for an international perspective.

To an American it might seem that Davie accomplished this Anglo-American rapprochement through his books. Until recently his critical reputation on this side of the Atlantic rested mainly on a quartet of groundbreaking full-length volumes: *Purity of Diction in English Verse* (1953); *Articulate Energy: An Enquiry into the Syntax of English Poetry* (1955); *Ezra Pound: Poet as Sculptor* (1964); and *Thomas Hardy and British Poetry* (1972). Poets and critics alike hailed these books as crucial reassessments of the Modern movement in English literature. His shorter work was less known and less available. Most of it was published in the United Kingdom, often in small magazines or scholarly journals, and until *The Poet in the Imaginary Museum,* it was never collected.

What one learns reading through this volume is that Davie is really at his best in short essays. His books have always had the tendency to break up into collections of brilliant but only partially related chapters. His recent book *Ezra Pound* (1976) is demonstrably a collection of discrete essays on Pound organized mainly by the chronology of the works Davie discusses. Yet this is hardly a damning criticism. The compact form of the essay or the essay-review is the right genre for exploring one idea or clarifying one point. If novels are currently preferred to short stories, and full-length studies to essays, it is due more to the economics of publishing and the politics of university promotions than to the hierarchy of literary forms. Most of the important poet-critics in English have favored shorter forms for criticism—Johnson, Coleridge, Arnold, Pound, Eliot, Auden, Jarrell—so it is hardly surprising that Davie would excel in this form.

The one major problem with *The Poet in the Imaginary Museum* is that it tries to do so many things at once that it cannot do them all well. This fault, however, lies more with the editor than with the author. Professor Alpert has let his enthusiasm get the better of his editorial judgment. While he has put together an excellent book, his unfocused editing has unfortunately served to obscure its real importance. The volume runs to over three hundred pages of closely set, small type. Quotations of verse are inelegantly jammed between prose paragraphs with no breathing space whatsoever. For those inclined to eyestrain it is as dangerous to read as the stock-exchange pages of the *New York Times.* Surely Davie deserves something slightly better. The editor should have faced the fact that it was impossible to represent more than a fraction of what an author as prolific as Davie has written. The short reviews whose interest now is mainly historical should have been omitted. For example, Davie's terse rejection of Randall Jarrell's poetry from *The Listener* in 1957 certainly does not add much either to the volume or to Davie's reputation as a reader of modern poetry. He simply dismisses Jarrell as a psychological case-writer without ever quoting a line of his poetry. An admirer of Jarrell's poetry would need a stronger case than that to change his or her mind. Equally disturbing is Davie's summary judgment of Roethke's *The Far Field* as "fatty, wasteful, and coarse." Perhaps Roethke's poetry does suffer from a vague "oceanic feeling," but is this still all there is to be said about it now? These short reviews and others do not belong in this volume. Good or bad, they are simply distracting from the book's real contributions to criticism. They should have been saved for the collection of Davie's occasional criticism which will certainly be printed someday.

There is no shortage of first-rate work in the volume, however, and many of the selections—including the title essay, as well as "T. S. Eliot: The End of an Era" and "American and English in *Briggflatts*"—seem destined for a central place in the study of modern poetry. Together the finest essays form a useful guide to twentieth-century poetry in English, and now that they are finally available in book form they will achieve the attention they deserve. *The Poet in the Imaginary Museum* will undoubtedly become required reading for all serious students of modern literature, but it would be a shame if this book's audience were exclusively academic. It is so rare nowadays that a major critic can speak so eloquently to the general reader that it would be distressing to discover that the right people are not listening.

Index

UNDER DISCUSSION
David Lehman, General Editor
Donald Hall, Founding Editor

Volumes in the Under Discussion series collect reviews and essays about individual poets. The series is concerned with contemporary American and English poets about whom the consensus has not yet been formed and the final vote has not been taken. Titles in the series include: